BADMINTON

About the authors

Two native Texans who acquired most of their education in the Lone Star State, Margaret Varner Bloss and Virginia A. Brown, have joined forces in this revision of Mrs. Bloss's original text. Both have achieved success in competitive sports, in teaching, and in writing. Their knowledge and experiences in racket sports blend exceptionally well together.

After earning her B.A. and M.A. degrees at Texas Woman's University, Margaret Varner Bloss devoted years to teaching physical education at the college level. She was twice World Badminton Champion and has won many other major badminton titles, including the U.S. Singles and Mixed Doubles, the All-England Ladies Doubles, and the World Invitation Ladies Doubles in Scotland. She has played on, captained, and coached U.S. Uber Cup and Wightman Cup Teams. She was Captain of the U.S. Touring Team—men and women—to South Africa. "The racket champion," she is the only woman who has represented the U.S.A. in international competition in three different racket sports—badminton, tennis, and squash racquets—the Uber cup, Wightman cup, and Wolfe-Noel cup, respectively. She is now married to W. Gerald Bloss and is the mother of two delightful children.

Following graduation from Baylor University and the obtaining of her M.Ed. from North Texas State University, Virginia A. Brown continues studying at various universities while teaching during academic semesters at Odessa, Texas schools. She has conducted numerous physical education demonstrations and workshops throughout the nation, and has, in addition, authored articles for numerous sports periodicals. Both her men's and women's tennis teams at Odessa College have won national collegiate championships, and she has guided her teams to ten consecutive Western Junior College Conference titles. Moreover, she has twice been named Coach of the Year in the Western Junior College Conference and is the only female coach to serve on the men's National Junior College Tennis Committee. Besides her coaching accomplishments, she is a former Texas Intercollegiate Badminton Champion and has competed in the Wimbledon tennis championships as well as the U.S. Nationals at Forest Hills. She is currently coach of both the men's and women's tennis teams at Odessa College and at the new University of Texas of the Permian Basin.

BADMINTON

Physical Education Activities Series

Margaret Varner Bloss
University of Texas, El Paso

Virginia A. Brown
Odessa College
and
University of Texas
of the Permian Basin

THIRD EDITION

Wm C Brown Company Publishers
Dubuque, Iowa

Consulting Editor

Aileene Lockhart
Texas Woman's University

Evaluation Materials Editor

Jane A. Mott
Smith College

Contents

Preface

This book is intended to provide both the beginning and the advanced badminton player with an organized description of how best to perform and enjoy the game. The real student of badminton must not only learn *how* to execute fundamental techniques but he should learn *when* and *why* they should be used. These specifics are discussed here. Instructions and analyses are accompanied by sequence photographs and illustrative diagrams. Practice drills are outlined. A glossary of terms peculiar to badminton, a section on equipment, a description of badminton associations and tournaments, and a bibliography together provide a handy reference source for the enthusiast. Supplemental material includes skill games, study questions, a section on officiating, and a sample score sheet.

Self-evaluation questions are distributed throughout the text. These afford the reader typical examples of the kinds of understanding and levels of skill that he should be acquiring as he progresses toward mastery of badminton. The player should not only answer the printed questions but should pose additional ones as a self-check on learning. Since the sequence for the reading of the textual content and the instructor's progression are both matters of individual decision, the evaluative materials are not positioned according to the presentation of given topics. In some instances the student may find that he cannot respond fully and accurately to a question until he has read more extensively or has gained more playing experience. From time to time he should return to such troublesome questions until he is sure of the answers or has developed the skills called for, as the case may be.

Although this book is designed primarily for college physical education classes, the information is clearly suitable for and useful to backyard, club, or tournament players.

What badminton is like

Badminton, a game which gets its name from an English estate, is played with rackets and shuttlecocks on a court divided by a net. It appears to have been played in India and England in the mid and late nineteenth century. However, since that time, the game has enjoyed considerable popularity in many countries. Always very well liked in the British Isles, badminton is considered virtually the national sport in their respective countries by India, Malaysia, Indonesia, and Thailand. Denmark, Sweden, and West Germany lead the European countries in their interest. The game spread to Canada and the United States where national organizations similar to those of other countries were formed. The number of clubs in the U.S. is, however, not comparable to the number found in the aforementioned countries. As leisure time increases, badminton will no doubt play an important role in the fitness and recreational programs so vital to the American citizen. It can be played by men, women, and children of all ages with a minimum of expense and effort. The game itself is stimulating mentally and physically, and it combines the values of individual and team sports. The fact that it can be learned easily makes it enjoyable from the outset. Basic techniques are easy to learn, yet much practice and concentration are required to perfect the skills needed for becoming a good player.

Badminton can be played indoors or outdoors, under artificial or natural lighting. There may be two players on a side (the four-handed or doubles game) or one player on a side (the two-handed or singles game). The shuttlecock does not bounce; therefore it is played in the air, making for an exceptionally fast game requiring quick reflexes and superb conditioning. There is a wide variety of strokes in the game ranging from powerfully hit smashes to delicately played dropshots.

The measurements of the singles and doubles courts are shown in figures 1.1 and 1.2. The court is bisected by a net elevated five feet above the ground at the center and one inch higher at the posts (5′ 1″), which are situated on the doubles sidelines. When the game is played indoors, the ceiling of the badminton hall should be not less than twenty-six feet from the floor over the full court area. This area should be entirely free of girders and other obstructions. There should be at least four feet of clear space surrounding each court and between any two courts. The shuttlecock (or shuttle) may be made of nylon or genuine feathers. It con-

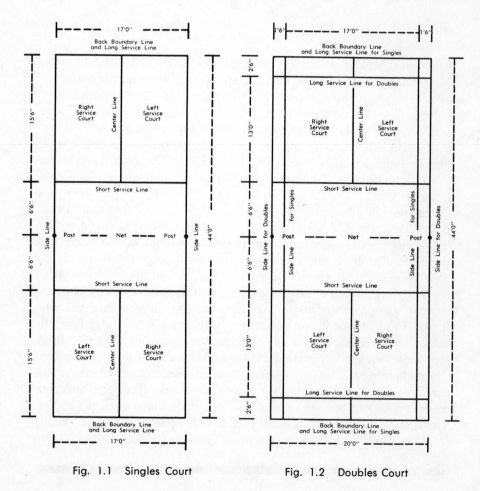

Fig. 1.1 Singles Court   Fig. 1.2 Doubles Court

sists of from fourteen to sixteen goose feathers and weighs from seventy-three to eighty-five grains. The racket is light in weight, only five ounces, and is strung with gut or nylon. Figure 1.3 shows a fine quality racket and shuttle.

A badminton game consists of 15 points, except in ladies singles which is 11 points. The best of three games constitutes a match. Occasionally a handicap game of 21 points is played, in which case one game completes a match. The right to choose ends or to either serve or receive first in the first game of a match is decided by the toss of a coin or the spin of a racket. See page 65. If the side winning the toss chooses to serve first, the other side chooses ends, and vice versa. The sides change ends at the beginning of the second game and at the beginning of the third if a third game is necessary. In a 15-point game, ends are changed in the third game when the leading side reaches 8; in an 11-point game when either side reaches 6, ends are changed. The side that wins a game serves first in the next game.

When the game is "13 all" in singles and doubles games which consist of 15 points, the side which reached 13 first has the option of "setting" the game to 5 (a total of 18 points), and the side that scores 5 points first wins the game. The score may be set in the same manner at "14 all" for 3 points (a total of 17 points). In ladies' singles, the 11-point game may total 12 points by setting at "9 all" for 3 points or "10 all" for 2 points. Turn to chapter 7 for a more detailed description of setting. Unlike table tennis, a game does not need to be won when a player leads by two points. For example, the score of a match could be 15-14, 15-13, 17-16.

The game is started with an underhand stroke (serve) by a player in the right service court serving to a player in the right service court diagonally opposite. After the serve is completed, the shuttle is "in play" back and forth across the net until it touches the ground, or goes into the net, or until some other fault occurs. Points can be scored only by the serving side. Unlike tennis, the server in badminton has only one attempt to put the shuttlecock into play.

In singles, if the server fails to win the point, the score remains the same; it is then "service over," and the opposing side gains the serve and the opportunity to score. When a player has scored an even number of points, the serve must be to the right service court; when the server's score is an odd number of points, the serve is always sent to the left service court. The receiver adjusts accordingly.

In doubles, only one partner of the side that starts a game has a turn at serving in the first inning; in every subsequent inning each player on each side has a turn, the partners serving consecutively. (In baseball, an inning refers to a team's turn at bat. In badminton both singles and doubles,

Fig. 1.3   Racket and Shuttlecock

an inning indicates a turn at serving for a player or players.) In doubles, when a point is scored, the server changes courts and serves to the other service court. Only the serving side changes service courts when a point is scored. The receivers remain in their same courts to allow the server to serve to the other player.

Badminton is a fun game because it is easy to play—the shuttlecock can be hit back and forth (rallies) even when the players possess a minimum of skill. Within a week or two after the beginning of a class, rallies and scoring can take place. There are very few sports in which it is possible to get the feeling of having become an "instant player." However, it is not to be assumed that perfection of strokes and tournament caliber of play is by any means less difficult in badminton than in other sports. A typical rally in badminton singles should consist of a serve, repeated high deep shots hit to the backline (clears) interspersed with dropshots. If and when a short clear or other type of "set-up" is forced, a smash wins the point. More often than not, an error (shuttle hit out-of-bounds or into the net) occurs rather than a positive playing finish to the rally. As a player's skill increases, he should commit fewer errors and make more outright winning plays to gain points. A player who is patient and commits few or no outright errors often wins despite the fact that he may not be spectacular. He simply waits for his opponent to err. That is badminton. In the doubles game there are fewer clears, more low serves, drives, and net play. (All of these terms are described in the next and succeeding chapters.) Again, the smash often terminates the point. As in singles, patience and the lack of unforced errors is most desirable. Team play and strategy in doubles is very important, and often two players who have perfected their doubles system (rotating up and back on offense and defense) can prevail over two superior stroke players lacking in sound doubles teamwork and strategy.

In addition to the service regulations described in this chapter there are other rules to follow in playing the game, and certain terms to understand; these specifics are discussed in chapters 6 and 7.

Skills essential
for everyone

2

Before attempting stroking technique, a player must learn how to grip his racket, where to position himself on the court, how to stand when awaiting returns, and how to move about the playing surface.

THE GRIPS (figs. 2.1 AND 2.2)

Most badminton strokes are executed with the use of either a forehand or backhand grip. Strokes made overhead or on the right side of the body require a forehand grip; strokes made on the left side of the body require a backhand grip. (These suggestions and instructions and others of a similar nature throughout the book pertain to right-handed players; left-handed players should in each case use the side opposite to that cited.)

The forehand grip in badminton resembles the Eastern forehand grip in tennis in that the point of the **V** formed by the thumb and forefinger is on the top bevel of the eight-sided handle. The top bevel is the side of the handle which is visible when the racket head is held perpendicular to the ground. In order to allow for wrist movement, hold the racket in the fingers rather than palming it. The handle lies diagonally across the fingers and palm allowing the little finger to maintain a firm hold. More wrist action is achieved if the racket is held as near the end of the handle as possible. The fingers, particularly the forefinger and third finger, are comfortably spread. Hold the racket firmly at impact when executing power shots and more loosely on "touch" shots.

To get a comfortable feeling it may be necessary to adjust this basic grip by spreading or closing the fingers, by moving the hand closer to the

Can you take a forehand grip and bounce the shuttle on the racket face without missing for 10, 15, and then 20 times?
With the same grip, can you alternate sides of the racket for each bounce?

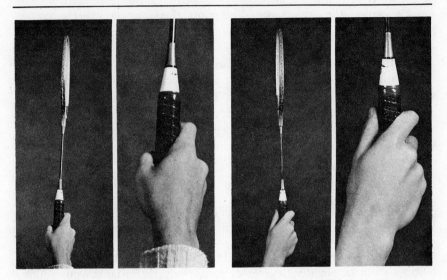

Fig. 2.1   Forehand Grip   Fig. 2.2   Backhand Grip

end, or by resting the end of the handle at a comfortable place on the heel of the hand. The position of the **V** should not change.

To take a backhand grip for shots played on the left side of the body, turn your hand counterclockwise until the point of the **V** is on the top left bevel. Most important, place the ball of the thumb flat against the back bevel of the handle. This thumb position gives the support needed to gain speed on drives and depth on clears. Since dropshots and net shots demand control rather than power, it is not necessary to have the thumb flat; in fact, the side of the thumb may rest along the back bevel as it does on the forehand.

POSITION ON THE COURT

Center Location

The center or basic position is that location on the court from which you are able to reach most shots easily. It is equidistant from the net and back boundary line and equidistant from the sidelines. If you establish yourself in this position, you command the best area for any maneuver. Your opponent will try to draw you from this basic center position by directing the shuttle to a corner, thereby compelling you to move from the center of the court. Then, if he takes advantage of his corner placement, he will quickly exploit the open space. You must therefore retrieve the corner shots but recover quickly in order to return to the center position and close the space that was momentarily open. The basic position may be altered to some degree, depending upon your abilities and depending upon the position on the court from which your opponent is returning the shuttle (See chapter 5—angle of return). The more experience you gain playing badminton, the easier it will be for you to anticipate the returns. You will soon learn your opponent's strengths and weaknesses as well as your own, and your center location will adjust accordingly.

Ready Position (fig. 2.3)

To ready yourself for each of your opponent's strokes, take a position in the center of the court and stand alertly with your weight evenly distributed on the balls of your feet. Your feet should be apart just enough to give good balance, and yet not so far apart that movement is restricted. Knees should be slightly flexed and easy, ready for instantaneous action. Your body is relaxed rather than stiff and upright. Both arms are carried in front of the body with the racket acting almost as a shield to keep the shuttle from getting past. The racket head is held up about shoulder height in front and away from the body to allow a swift strike. Experiment to determine the best position for you. Your eyes concentrate on the shuttle as it is leaving your opponent's racket, endeavoring to ascertain the direction of the attack or defense. As soon as the direction is determined, your feet move, and your body is pivoting by the time the shuttle crosses the net.

Fig. 2.3   Ready Position

All players vary the ready position somewhat to suit their own style and comfort; champions adjust it to give them the greatest mobility and quickness. Quickness refers not only to feet and hands but to eyes and brain as well. The shuttle has such a short distance to travel that it will come swiftly and offer you little time to execute the fundamentals. In fact, in badminton there is absolutely no time to pause and "survey" the situation. Even in doubles, where your partner covers half of the court, you have to be ready for every shot. Points are made because opponents have neither the time nor the reflexes to get their rackets in position to return the shuttle.

FOOTWORK

In order to get within reach of the shuttlecock, good footwork is essential. Powerful and deceptive strokes are of little use if a player is not in the correct place soon enough to stroke the shuttle effectively.

The beginning of good footwork is an alert starting position. Keep the body ready to move in any direction by flexing the knees slightly with the weight on the forward part of the feet and think "ready." A stiff upright stance does not indicate or permit speed. "Bouncing" best describes badminton footwork.

To move to the baseline, take a sideways skipping action with the feet kept close to the floor. To hit a forehand or overhead stroke in the deep right court, skip diagonally back to your right, with the right foot leading, and finish with the left side partially turned toward the net with the left foot forward. To play a backhand drive or clear from the deep left court, skip diagonally back, left foot leading, and with the right side to the net and the right foot diagonally forward.

Since it is a natural habit, the easiest part of badminton footwork is running forward. Because the basic waiting position is in the center of the court, however, backward and sideward steps are also required. The skill of moving backwards is called "backpedaling." It is a talent demanded in other sports, too. The "T" formation quarterback backpedals almost every time he takes the ball from center. His success as a quarterback is greatly dependent on his ability to move backwards without turning around; so it is with the badminton player. The head and eyes should be forward at all times. If a player has to turn and run with his back to the net, he will not have enough time to turn again to stroke the shuttle with ease. In fact, he will have to struggle to make the shot before it contacts the court.

Good footwork combined with early anticipation of the direction and depth of the shuttlecock should place the player *behind* the shuttle, thus enabling a move forward and a hit into the shot. Sluggish footwork often results in the shuttle getting behind the player, resulting in a poorly executed stroke. Good footwork is not only important in returning high deep clears but essential for an effective return of a high deep serve.

THE STROKES

The basic badminton strokes are the serve, the overhead clear, the dropshot, the overhead smash, and the drive. To play shots close to the net on the backhand side, stroke with the right foot placed forward and the right side to the net. This position is the same as on all backhand shots. On the forehand side, either the right foot or the left foot may be extended to meet the shuttle. The choice may depend on how far the player has had to move to reach the shuttlecock. By extending the right foot on the forehand side a few inches are added to a player's reach. Try it and see. After playing a shot at net, the player should move back to the center position without turning around. Keep facing the net with your eye on the shuttle at all times.

Note figure 2.4. Except for the serve, which is an underhand stroke, and the drive, which is a sidearm stroke, the overhead stroke preparations of the clear, drop, and smash should be as indistinguishable as possible.

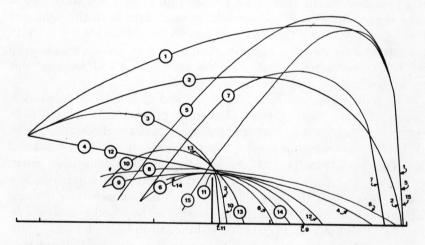

1. Defensive Clear	6. Low Doubles Serve	11. Hairpin Net Shot
2. Attacking Clear	7. High Doubles Serve	12. Half-Smash
3. Overhead Dropshot	8. Drive	13. Net Smash
4. Smash	9. Midcourt Drive	14. Push Shot
5. High Singles Serve	10. Underhand Dropshot	15. Underhand Clear

Fig. 2.4 Flight Patterns

The fun of many games is to make use of the basic elements (strokes, in badminton) in such a way (strategy) that you outwit and deceive your opponent. Keep this in mind from the very beginning as you learn the strokes. Badminton is a game that epitomizes deception and your strokes should reflect this characteristic.

Your game will develop and grow, and your potential can be fulfilled sooner if thought and attention are given to the basic instructions in this chapter. Attention to detail is a characteristic of the champion.

The Serve (fig. 2.5)

The serve is the underhand stroke that begins play. Legally it can be played underhand forehand or underhand backhand, although underhand forehand is the usual method. The shaft of the racket must now point downwards so that the whole of the head of the racket is discernibly below the hand holding the racket. (See figure 7.2, p. 68.)

Basic Singles Serve   To serve in singles, take a comfortable position in the court about three feet behind the short service line and to the right or left of the centerline. Stand with your feet spread but not so far apart that you cannot move quickly. The left foot should be in advance of the right. A player's feet must remain in contact with the floor until the shuttle is contacted. Once the racket is put in motion to serve, neither foot may

Fig. 2.5   Serve

slide during the entire execution of the stroke. Hold the shuttle at the base between the thumb and forefinger of the left hand and extend the arm out at about shoulder level. The racket is held with a forehand grip with the wrist cocked and brought up behind the body at about waist level. This is the starting position; then the shuttle is dropped. The racket swings forward to the contact point at about knee level. Let the racket and shuttle meet ahead of and away from the body. The follow-through goes in the direction that you intend the shuttle to go. It will finish high since it is an underhand stroke and the shuttle must be hit up and over the net. A common mistake, made especially by beginners, is in bringing the racket up to the shuttle without dropping the shuttle. Such practice results in an outright miss or in a wood shot.

Dropping shuttle too close to body   Contacting shuttle on too high a plane

Fig. 2.6   Mistakes Most Commonly Made with the Low Serve

The Low Serve   The low serve is used almost exclusively in doubles and with great variation. The grips and stance are usually the same as for the singles serve, but the racket pattern and use of the wrist are almost indescribable. Of all the strokes in badminton, the low serve technique has the most variables. The swing is often shortened and the stroke made almost entirely with the wrist. Other players prefer an exceptionally firm wrist believing it gives more control. This is one stroke a player must experiment with and find the style best suited for him. Try for accuracy in having the shuttle go over the top of the net with minimum clearance. If your low serve forces the receiver to hit up it is a highly successful serve. If the receiver "rushes" your low serve and is able to hit it on the downswing, change your technique and practice it more.

Backhand Serve   The backhand serve has been used in the past primarily by Asian players. It may be served low or flicked. The right foot should be forward, the racket held with a backhand grip, and the shuttle held in front of the body close to the racket. This serve is useful because the white shuttle is difficult to see when held in front of white clothing, and it is easy to flick a backhand—both of these points adding to the deceptiveness of the stroke. <u>A low serve hitting the top of the net and falling into the correct service court is legal and "in play."</u>

Placement Areas (fig. 2.7)   As shown in figure 2.4, the serve can be directed high or low, short or long. Figure 2.7 shows the specific areas within the service court to which the shuttle can be served most effectively. In singles there should be no noticeable difference in the way one produces low and high serves, as here again deception is important in order to keep your opponent in doubt as to which it will be (and off balance). Basically, the high serve is used more often in singles and the low serve more often in doubles. Occasionally mixing them keeps your opponent uncertain and unable to predict your pattern. It is imperative that you serve well, as serving gives you the opportunity to score.

Even though somewhat alike in production, the low and high serves are very different. They can be compared with the dropshot and clear as regards wrist action and needed power. The low serve takes little power and is almost guided over the net whereas the high, deep serve will take all the strength and power available to get it high enough and deep enough to be considered successful. It has much the same flight as the clear be-

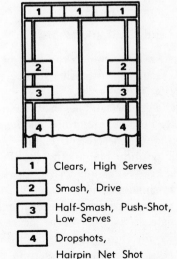

Fig. 2.7 Placement Areas

1 Clears, High Serves

2 Smash, Drive

3 Half-Smash, Push-Shot, Low Serves

4 Dropshots, Hairpin Net Shot

cause it is hit to a point high above the backcourt, and when it loses its speed, it turns and falls straight down. If it falls straight down on the back boundary line, the opponent must be that far back in the court to return it. If it is too flat and too low, the receiver will intercept it before it ever gets to the backcourt. On the other hand, the low serve has a flat arc as it just skims over the net and into the court near the short service line. The low serve in doubles requires the same grip and foot position. However, the backswing is shortened, the shuttle contacted as near waist level as possible, and perhaps slightly more to the right. The shuttle is guided over the net without wrist motion. A great deal less shoulder, arm, and wrist power will be needed to hit the short distance and low trajectory required for the low serve.

Because the serve is played underhand and therefore must be hit upward, it is considered a defensive stroke. Consequently, in order to score, the server must eventually turn his defense into an attack. Since the receiver cannot score a point, his objective is to stay on the attack and win the opportunity to serve, making it possible then for him to score. This peculiarity of badminton—having to score from a beginning defensive position—prolongs a game even though no points are recorded. Championship matches often illustrate this. In 1952, for example, two leading international players, Dave Freeman of the United States and Wong Peng Soon of Malaya played a Thomas Cup singles match. The final score was 15/4, 15/1 and the match took over an hour to complete. The players must have been in superb physical condition and evenly matched, despite the fact that the final score gives no indication as to how close the match actually was.

The Overhead Clear (fig. 2.8)

<u>The clear is a high shot to the back of the court; it may be offensive or defensive.</u> Generally, offensive shots are hit down. The attacking clear is the exception to this rule.

To get a good clear, take the proper forehand grip, watch the approaching shuttle, use the prescribed footwork, and move yourself to a place where you are in the correct relationship to the shuttle. As you are moving to this position behind the shuttle, swing your racket and arm back behind the head and shoulders. This will require pivoting at the waist and turning the shoulders sideways to the net. The position is fundamentally the same as that taken by a baseball outfielder making an overarm throw to home plate. In badminton the racket, instead of the ball, is in the hand, but it is literally thrown at the shuttle in the identical fashion. The forearm rotates as the racket moves from behind the head, and the arm becomes fully extended at the contact point. Incorrectly allowing the arm to drop and bend when stroking results in loss of power. In addition, the extended arm gives great freedom of movement and the uninhibited and satisfying feeling of good clean stroking. The trunk is rotated forward to gain needed power. The contact point is not directly above the head as overhead might imply; it is in front of you. Your ideal position is behind and in line with the shuttle. Overheads should be taken ahead at the nearest possible point of contact, and not be allowed to drop low and to the side. Consequently, always hit the shuttle as soon as possible so that your opponent will not have time to get to your shots. Meet the shuttle with a flat racket or surface without any cutting or slicing motion. Cutting gives control but takes away power.

In badminton, power is essential to send the clear high and deep. In addition, the shuttlecock is difficult to slice because of its feathers, and it does not react as a spinning ball does. Since you want the shuttle to go high and deep, the racket will swing forward and up, and the follow-through will simply follow the shuttle. In many strokes the purpose of the follow-through is to bring the shuttle down—but not in this instance. It could almost be said that there is no follow-through. The racket might finish pointing down because of the wrist snap, but the arm is not brought down purposely. The contact of the racket and shuttle must be quite explosive to get distance, since there is little weight in the racket. The angle of the racket face upon contact is the final determining factor as to the direction the shuttle will take. Be sure to move your weight into the shot as the stroke is made. Note the flight pattern of the clear in figure 2.4. The shuttle is hit high enough so that at a certain point, almost above the back boundary line, it loses speed and turns and falls straight down. A shuttle falling perpendicular to the floor is most difficult to play. Very few people have power enough to smash a clear from the back boundary line. By the time the smash reaches the other side of the net, its speed has greatly diminished.

The high deep or defensive clear is used primarily to gain time for the player to return to the center position in the court. One of the most valuable benefits of this shot is derived from its use in combinations with the dropshot to run your opponent, making him defend all four corners of the court.

As can be seen in figure 2.4, depth and height of the shuttlecock on the defensive clear are extremely important in order to force your opponent as far into the backcourt as possible. Your next shot, a dropshot just over the net, would become very effective in this game of maneuvering for openings and spaces. It might also force your opponent to hit a short return which could be smashed. It takes a strong player to clear from one baseline to the opposite one and an extraordinarily strong player to high

Fig. 2.8   Overhead Clear

Hitting with bent arm   Failure to contact shuttle in front of body

Fig. 2.9   Mistakes Most Commonly Made with the Overhead Clear

Can you and your opponent rally the shuttle for fifteen, twenty, and then twenty-five consecutive hits?

clear to the diagonal corner. Unless a shuttle that flies very fast is used, it is unlikely that the average player would be able to accomplish this difficult feat. Consequently, in singles, the player who first hits a high deep defensive clear gains control of the rally and should eventually win that point. In analyzing a match played by contestants of equal skill, the player who consistently has good length always wins. When playing, if you find you do not have time to reach the shots and each point is a struggle, then check the length of your clears. Your opponent will seldom return a winning shot or putaway if your clear is deep enough. Clears that are too low and too short are cut off before they reach the backcourt.

After learning the basic high deep clear just described, a modification of this shot, the attacking clear, can be developed. Its use should not be confused with the uses of the defensive clear or disaster will result. The trajectory of the attacking clear is not as high but it is faster. There is a different arc to the flight pattern, as can be seen in figure 2.4. Because it is low, the opponent must be drawn out of the center position before the attacking clear can be used successfully. Often it is best used following a good dropshot to the forehand corner. The clear can then be hit quickly to the backhand corner while the opponent is recovering from the net. Once the clear gets behind the opponent on the backhand, the return is almost sure to be in the forecourt. When an opponent's return is forced to be short, the point should be yours! A defensive clear incorrectly used in this situation would give the opponent time to move back and hit overhead, and the advantage would be lost.

The only difference in the production of these two types of clears is that the attacking clear has a flatter arc; therefore stroke it with less upward angle. It also requires less power, since without the height there is less distance to travel. Care must be taken when standing near the net that the flat clear is not sent out over the back boundary line. It necessitates controlled power and yet it has to be fast enough to get behind the opponent.

The Dropshot (fig. 2.10)

The dropshot is a slow shot that drops just over the net in the opponent's forecourt. To produce it, use exactly the same grip, footwork, body position, and backswing described for the overhead clear. Indeed, your intention should be to suggest that a clear is forthcoming. The difference lies in wrist speed. There is still full wrist movement, but the shuttle is stroked with great control rather than "patted." The shuttle must be contacted farther ahead of the body than is the clear and with an extended arm in order to direct it downwards. The downward movement of the arm coupled with the completion of the wrist action brings the shuttle down. In addition, the face of the racket is tilted downward at the angle you wish the shuttle to take. The shoulders and trunk are rotated forward and the weight moves into the shot.

A dropshot is invaluable because it enables you to use the front corners of the court. No other type of shot goes to the two front corners near the net. The smash and drive are placed midcourt or deeper, as shown in figure 2.7. The clear is always placed in the backcourt; therefore, in order to make full use of the court and to move your opponent, the two front corners cannot be neglected. The dropshot, whether overhead, underhand, or hit from the side and from any place on the court, fills this need.

A major part of singles strategy lies in the use of the overhead dropshot in combination with clears. For example, if clears are used repeatedly,

Fig. 2.10   Dropshot

a player tends to move his basic position towards the rear of the court in order to cover the deep shots. This makes the dropshot doubly effective. Singles becomes a game of up and back and up and back again until a weak return is forced and a smash finishes the rally. A midcourt shot, one which is halfway between the net and back boundary line, obviously is not as useful in singles as in doubles, since these shots do not move the opponent out of center. Consequentiy, keep the shuttle as far from the center of the court as possible with clears and drops. The underhand clear and underhand dropshot are described in chapter 3.

The most outstanding characteristic of a good dropshot is its deception. If the dropshot is deceptive enough it can be an outright winner even though it might have been planned as a lead-up shot. If it is obvious to your opponent that a dropshot is forthcoming, the play will not be difficult for him even though the drop has been accurately placed in a front corner. If your opponent is halfway to the net or at the net before your shot reaches the net, then you haven't fooled him!

The least attractive characteristic of the dropshot is its slow flight. Anything moving slowly unfortunately gives your opponent what you don't want him to have—time. The drop must be extremely accurate, then, to be effective. If your opponent anticipates the drop and has time to reach it, you have probably lost the exchange. It will take only a second for

Incorrect angle of racket face   Failure to follow through

Fig. 2.11 Mistakes Most Commonly Made with the Dropshot

your adversary to get the shuttle back over on your side of the net. The dropshot then, contributes to the essence of the game—the selection of particular shots based on measuring time in relation to your own and your opponent's position on the court.

The Smash (fig. 2.12)

The smash is a powerful overhead shot used to "put away" any shuttle above the height of the net.

In the interest of deception, the smash should be masked as a clear or a drop. Use the same grip, footwork, body position, backswing, and contact point as with the clear and the drop, and your opponent will not anticipate your return. The smash differs from the clear and the dropshot in that it can be hit only from an overhead position; a clear and a dropshot can be either an overhead or underhanded shot. Be sure you move yourself to a position behind the shuttle as quickly as possible. Take care to have a proper body position, since balance must be perfect to achieve maximum power from your shoulders, arms, and wrist. The left shoulder must be turned to the net and the right shoulder back and ready to strike with force. The arm and wrist are cocked behind the body ready to unleash all available power. The racket head may be moving at a terrific rate as it goes out to meet the shuttle. The handle must be gripped quite firmly at the instant of contact, and the shuttle contacted at the highest possible point. The follow-through is down and in line with the flight of the shuttle. The overhead smash should be hit with as much power as that needed for the high, deep clear. To get such power, the wrist action must be full and the timing perfect. The trunk and shoulders are rotated forward and the weight is thrown into the shot. When you are first learning to smash, however, try to get your timing and downward angle correct before attempting to get excessive speed. Timing is thrown off if too much arm and body effort are involved in the stroke.

The racket face must be angled downward at contact point to make the shuttle travel sharply downward. It is important to remember that the farther away you are from the net the less angle to the floor you can get. Important, too, is that the farther you are from the net when you smash, the less speed your smash will have when it reaches your opponent's midcourt.

There are two reasons for using a smash. First, because it has more downward angle and speed than any other stroke, it is the main point-winning shot. If the pattern of play has developed as planned, your final stroke of the rally will be an overhead smash. Second, if the smash is returned, the return will be, because of the angle of your smash, an upward (defensive) stroke. Obviously, in both situations the smash is an

Fig. 2.12   Smash

Failure to get behind shuttle   Failure to get in line with shuttle

Fig. 2.13   Mistakes Most Commonly Made with the Smash

invaluable weapon. There is, however, a reason for avoiding indiscriminate use of the smash; namely, the effort needed to smash leaves the body off balance, and therefore it takes longer to recover your position than with other types of shots. Moreover, repeated smashing is tiring and reveals weak thinking. So your judgment as to when to smash rather than to clear or to drop is important. Many factors related to you and to your opponent will enter into this decision.

It is interesting to note the characteristics which are alike in making the various shots. See figures 2.8 and 2.10. The position of the feet and body is the same for all overhead shots. The stroke pattern—backswing, forward swing, and follow-through—should also be almost identical for the overhead strokes in order to employ the deception necessary to make the shots effective. What, then, determines whether an overhead shot is to be a clear, a dropshot, or a smash? The answer lies in the speed of the wrist, the degree of wrist action used, and the angle of the face of the racket at the moment of contact with the shuttle. On all badminton shots, cock the wrist back ready for the action that comes within the larger action of the shoulder and arm swing. Wrist power alone is not sufficient to propel the shuttle from one end of the court to the other; it necessitates arm power and shoulder rotation in addition to exact timing of the wrist snap as the weight moves forward. When a player intends to smash and put the shuttle "away," he may leap off the ground for better angle and possible added power. In this case, he is not using any deception to enhance the stroke. Total energy is being called upon instead.

Angle of the Racket Face   The direction of the shuttle's flight in all overhead shots is determined by the angle of the racket face. Bringing the wrist and racket head through too soon causes an extreme downward angle to the shuttle, often resulting in a netted shot. Conversely, failure to bring the wrist and racket head through soon enough causes an extreme upward angle. See the illustration below.

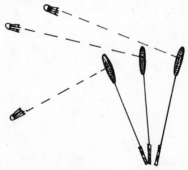

The Drives (figs. 2.14 and 2.15)

The drive is a flat sidearm stroke played as a forehand or backhand.

The forehand drive is played on the right side of the body and is similar to the baseball sidearm throw. Take a forehand grip, turn your body until the left side is to the net, place the left foot diagonally forward, and turn the shoulders to allow the arm to take the backswing. The backswing is taken by placing the head of the racket between your shoulder blades. To do this, bend your elbow and cock your wrist backward in preparation for a big, full, powerful swing. Watch the shuttle closely with the idea of contacting it diagonally ahead of your left foot. As your arm and racket swing forward, your body weight should transfer from the right foot to the left foot, your wrist uncock, and your arm straighten out at the point of contact. Contact the shuttle with a flat racket well away from you so that your swing is not restricted. The racket swings on through in the direction of the flight of the shuttle. The speed of your swing compels the racket to complete its follow-through by the left shoulder. The racket has practically made a 360° circle. The action of the swing, particularly in the contact area, is explosive.

The backhand drive employs the same basic principles as the forehand drive with two or three exceptions. The grip is changed to the backhand grip, making sure that the thumb is flat on the handle in order to give the extra support and snap that are needed. With this backhand grip there is less wrist action on the left side of the body and the wrist can be taken back only half as much as on the forehand side. The range of elbow movement is increased by this grip, however. This action of the elbow is important in this and all other strokes. On the backswing the elbow is bent, the right hand is at the left shoulder, and the elbow is pointing at the oncoming shuttle. The weight shifts, the shoulders turn, the arm starts swinging forward with the elbow leading, and then the head of the racket whips through for the contact and follow-through.

Long, deep, fast drives and slower paced midcourt drives can be played from either side of the body. Drives can be played like other shots, from one sideline diagonally across the court to the other sideline (crosscourt) or they can be played parallel to the sideline (down-the-line). The flight pattern of the drive is parallel to the floor and just skims the net. See figure 2.4. The drive is played anywhere from midcourt to backcourt and is driven to the opponent's midcourt or backcourt depending on his location in the court at the moment.

The higher you can contact the shuttle on the drive, the less you will have to hit up. For example, if you hit the shuttle from below knee level, it will have to go up to get over the net and will continue to rise as it

Fig. 2.14 Forehand Drive

Failure to rotate shoulders before stroking   Failure to meet shuttle soon enough

Fig. 2.15   Mistakes Most Commonly Made with the Forehand Drive

Fig. 2.16 Backhand Drive

Failure to rotate shoulders before stroking   Failure to meet shuttle soon enough

Fig. 2.17 Mistakes Most Commonly Made with the Backhand Drive

carries on to midcourt. If it rises to net level and then turns toward the floor because the speed is lost, you have mistakenly hit a dropshot. Any shot higher than net level can be smashed and therein lies the danger of the hard hit drive played from a low contact point. A drive less powerful (midcourt) may be of value if the opponent is not pulled out of position. Its arc will reach its peak at the net and descend from there on to midcourt. It therefore cannot be smashed.

The fast drive is used when an opponent is out of position and you wish to get the shuttle behind him to the backcourt. Perhaps you hit a well-placed dropshot to his forehand. The deep backhand corner is now briefly open. If your opponent returns your dropshot to your forehand, your problem is simple. If he plays it down-the-line to your backhand, it is not so simple. You must get the shuttle there quickly before he gains the center of the court or he will block the shot off for a winner while you are still recovering from the execution of the stroke. It takes more time to recover body balance and center position from hard hit power shots than from dropshots, midcourt drives, or net shots.

If the two kinds of drives are used correctly and intelligently, they can be valuable attacking weapons. Used badly, they can cause disaster.

Angle of the Racket Face   The direction of the shuttle's flight is determined by the angle of the racket face. It will require a great deal of practice to learn to control the moment of impact of the racket head and the shuttle in order to direct shots down-the-line or crosscourt.

The Backhand Clear (fig. 2.18)

The backhand clear is a high, deep shot played from the left side of the court. Use the backhand grip with the ball of the thumb flat against the back bevel as described for the backhand drive. The feet and body positions are also identical with the drive. At the completion of the backswing, the elbow should be pointing at the oncoming shuttle. The most important aspect of the swing is the timing of the wrist as it swings the head of the racket forward to meet the shuttle (at just the right instant). Be sure to rotate the trunk and shoulders into the shot.

For many players, the backhand clear from deep court is the most difficult of all the shots. Excellent timing and power are essential to clear the shuttle high enough and deep enough to make it a safe shot. The high deep shot to the left side of the court could be played with a round-the-head shot or overhead clear, but the player's court position would be sacrificed. A player must assess his own capabilities before selecting the particular stroke for use.

Fig. 2.18   Backhand Clear

Failure to rotate shoulders   Failure to elevate elbow on backswing

Fig. 2.19   Mistakes Most Commonly Made with the Backhand Clear

With all strokes, the learning process is the slow, gradual one of getting increased accuracy, further depth, and additional speed. As you continue to play and practice, the shuttle will travel increasingly more often in the direction in which you aim it. You will attain more and more power in clears and smashes and (desirably) less and less speed in dropshots. To further help you stroke your shots effectively and with care, correctly executed basic positions and footwork must precede the actual stroke production. The entire process, then, is one of smooth coordination.

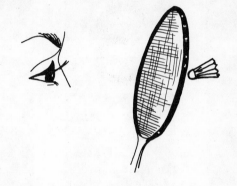

In every sport involving eye-hand contact, there is one fundamental principle which cannot be overemphasized. In the case of golf or tennis it is "keep your eye on the ball." In badminton it is "keep your eye on the shuttlecock." If you do not watch the shuttlecock, one of the following mistakes will probably occur:

1. You will miss the shuttlecock entirely.
2. You will hit the feathers of the shuttlecock.
3. You will not hit the shuttle in the center of the racket, thus causing a throw, sling, or a carry.

Better players
master these techniques

It is fun to experiment with additional strokes in combination with the essential skills described in chapter 2. Descriptions of supplementary shots, such as the half-smash, the round-the-head shot, the driven serve, the net shots (hairpin net shot, push shot, smash), and the underhand shots (clear, dropshot) will be found in this chapter. Many of these strokes are no more difficult to execute than the basic ones, but the learning of them should follow the mastery of sound basic strokes. Players who spend a great deal of time practicing the supplementary shots before mastering the fundamentals become chagrined when such practice fails to bring victory in tournament play. Often this dilemma is the result of dwelling on a spectacular, fancy shot or shots requiring less physical effort, rather than on standard, traditional shots which should be used the greater part of the time.

Nevertheless, as you gain experience and perfect your basic strokes, you will want to add the following accessory strokes to your repertoire. The value of employing these strokes is that they constitute an added threat, that is, they could be used any time. The fact that your opponent must be alert to this possibility further assures the effectiveness of the basic strokes.

ACCESSORY STROKES

The Half-Paced Smash

The half-paced smash, popularly called "half-smash," is simply a smash with less speed. The elements of stroke production related to the smash,

Can you smash 5 out of 10 of your opponent's high serves to midcourt?
Can you smash 8 out of 10 clears received at midcourt or deeper?

described in chapter 2 and figures 2.4 and 2.7, apply to the "half-smash." It is important to keep the following points in mind. The half-smash is played by contacting the shuttle with an extended arm diagonally above the head in order to obtain a steep angle downwards. To cut or slice the half-smash diminishes its speed and makes the shuttle fall close to the net at a sharper angle. If the shuttle gets behind the player, the racket will be facing upward at contact point, the flight of the shuttle will be upward, and the shot will be a defensive one, in all probability a clear. It is important, therefore, that the shuttle be contacted well ahead of the body. Caution: a smash hit with a bent arm results in loss of power and angle. The smash is then known as a "flat" smash, a highly undesirable shot.

The half-smash has as many values as the full, powerful smash, but is of a different nature. The half-smash can be played with less effort. Moreover, it can be played from deeper in the court since recovery of balance does not present a problem. Moving to cover the net return after the half-smash can be accomplished with ease. By contrast, a full smash from the backcourt leaves the front corners vulnerable. The use of the half-smash therefore is less risky. It is valuable, too, because of its sharply angled downward direction. By hitting downward, the attack is gained by forcing the opponent to stroke upward. Very few points are won outright from an underhand stroke. The ones that are can be attributed to outright deception or to outpositioning the opponent.

Backhand Smash

The backhand smash is an advanced stroke, but fun for beginning and intermediate players to at least try. The mechanics of the stroke are the same as for the clear and dropshot although the contact point must be forward and the racket face angled down. Probably its greatest value lies in element of surprise produced.

The Round-the-Head Shot (fig. 3.1)

The round-the-head shot is another overhead shot and an unusual one because it is played on the left or backhand side of the body. It may be a clear, a half-smash, or a dropshot. The execution of the round-the-head stroke is closely related to that of overhead strokes. See chapter 2 for instructions. One major difference, however, is that the contact point is above the left shoulder, necessitating a reach to the left and a bend of the knees and body. The shot is played with the body facing the net and the weight on the left foot and the palm of the hand facing the net when the racket contacts the shuttle. The right leg and weight swing forward for the follow-through of the stroke. The description and execution of the round-the-head stroke make it seem more difficult than it actually is.

Many sound reasons can be found for taking the shuttlecock with a round-the-head stroke rather than with a backhand stroke. First, more power is possible overhead than on the backhand, which, in turn, results in better depth and speed on the shuttle. In addition, since the opponent will be attacking the backhand corner, it is imperative that the area be protected at every opportunity. The round-the-head shot meets this need. For example, if a low clear or driven serve to the backhand side can be anticipated, it can be intercepted with a round-the-head shot.

Fig. 3.1   Round-the-Head Shot

Not all the results of this shot are favorable, however, as the feet and body will have to be moved to the left side of the court to guard the backhand area, and a large portion of the forehand side of the court will be left open. Advantages gained by this maneuver will have to be weighed

Failure to take weight on left leg   Failure to bend left knee and
while stroking   waist during stroke

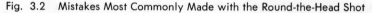

Fig. 3.2   Mistakes Most Commonly Made with the Round-the-Head Shot

against disadvantages. The strength of your backhand and your speed of foot will be determining factors in selecting the round-the-head instead of the backhand. The ideal player will be able to play the high backhand shot as well as the round-the-head shot.

The Driven Serve

A weak return is the desired outcome of a good driven serve. Sheer speed and force of shot will not be enough for success. The deceptive element must be present. Very few points are won outright on the driven serve, or on any serve, since it is played from an underhand (defensive) position. If the driven serve can jolt your opponent off balance and thus place you in an offensive position, the immediate objective has been achieved.

The mistake made by an ambitious receiver upon returning a good driven serve is to try to do too much with it. If the shuttle has carried behind the receiver as the server has planned it, the receiver should be content to play a safe, high, deep clear in order to regain balance. This serve will not be so effective if your opponent's speed of reflexes is exceptionally good. Against a player of different capabilities or against a player whose court position is faulty, the driven serve may be the answer to a serving problem.

The driven serve, most frequently used in doubles, has a specific value to a side-by-side (defensive) team. The angle that can be attained by serving from a position near the sideline can make an aggressive return almost impossible.

In conclusion, the effectiveness of the driven serve is due to its angle, speed, and some degree of deception. It must be noted here that the deception must be in the wrist. Any preliminary movements of the body intended to fool the receiver are illegal on the serve. If the server delays hitting the shuttle for so long as to be unfair to the receiver, it is a fault. This faulty tactic, called a balk, is further described in the rules in chapter 7.

NET PLAY

Net play is a general term encompassing those shots played from the area around the short service line to the net. See figure 2.4. Net play, which includes the hairpin net shot, the push shot, and the smash, is very important because the front of the court has to be defended.

The forehand grip described in chapter 2 is generally satisfactory for net play, but the backhand grip must be adjusted slightly. The side of the thumb is placed up the back bevel of the racket which may cause a slight turning of the hand toward the forehand grip. The wrist is used differently for net shots, that is, with little relationship to the shoulders and body. This grip adjustment allows such wrist action. On the other hand, this grip could not be used successfully to perform a clear from the backhand corner. On both forehand and backhand strokes, spread the fingers and hold the racket almost loosely. This should give more "touch." To get even more control, hold the racket slightly up from the end. This shortening of the grip gives less power (not needed at net) and less reach. You must decide, therefore, what you wish to gain (control) and what you wish to sacrifice (reach).

The feet, body, and upper arm are used for reaching rather than for stroke production; the actual strokes are done with the forearm, wrist, and hand. The racket meets the shuttle with a flat face. The wrist action may be smooth and controlled or it may be quick, depending on the type of net shot you are attempting. The explosive power so essential for clears and smashes is not needed in the forecourt.

The follow-through should be in the direction in which you wish the shuttle to travel. Guide it and go with it. At times, the follow-through must be abbreviated to avoid hitting the net. According to the rules, a player may not hit the net as long as the shuttle is in play. It is in play until it hits the net or floor.

Your court position for net play in singles and doubles should be such that your extended arm and racket can just touch the net. This distance from the net will permit unrestricted movement of your arm. In doubles it will also enable you to cover more midcourt shots.

In net play take fast, small steps which allow you to turn and move quickly in any direction. The left foot should be forward on forehand shots and the right foot on the backhand ones. In exceptional cases, the right foot may be forward when that extra bit of reach is needed to get to the shuttle on the forehand side.

The most difficult shots to play at net are those which are falling perpendicular to the floor rather than diagonally. Diagonally dropping shuttles arrive farther back in the court; perpendicular falling shuttles, at their best, touch or almost touch the net as they fall toward the floor. These are extremely difficult to play, and since they cannot be directed forward, only upward, they are called hairpin net shots. Your opponent, sensing this, is alert to smash as soon as the shuttle comes up and over the net.

Hairpin Net Shot   The hairpin net shot gets its name from the flight pattern of the shuttle. See figure 2.4. Played from one side of the net to the other, it should fall perpendicular to the floor and close to the net on the opponent's side. This shot travels the least distance of any badminton shot; consequently, very little stroke is needed. The shuttle played at net level may be tapped or blocked back. Played well below net level, it will have to be stroked with great care up and over the net. Some championship players stroke the shuttle with a slicing action which gives the shuttle less speed and a spinning motion that is difficult to return. The perfect hairpin shot results in the shuttle's crawling up and over the net and trickling down the other side.

Push Shot   The push shot is just what the name implies—a push, not a stroke. It is played at or above net level with the head of the racket up and the face of the racket flat. Its direction is angled downward. Refer to figure 2.4 in chapter 2.

The use of the push shot, almost nonexistent in singles, becomes highly effective in doubles. When a doubles team takes an up-and-back formation, the shot should be pushed down with a medium amount of speed to the opponent's midcourt. This will place the shuttle just behind the net player and force the backcourt player to reach and stroke the shuttle up. Confusion often results as to which player should return this shot. Obviously the push shot cannot be played from below net level.

Smash   The other highly important net shot that has to be played above net level is the smash. The shot is accomplished by a downward snap of the wrist. It is the best return of a high, short shot; it is the kill! Care must be taken not to get excessively enthusiastic at the prospect of a set-up and bang the shuttle or your racket into the net. Instead, keep your eye on the shuttle and control your swing until the point is completed. The direction of the smash at this close range is not important. If directed straight to the floor with great speed, the smash will be unreturnable. See figure 2.4.

Those net shots just described are used more frequently in doubles than in singles, but a good singles player's game is not complete without highly controlled net shots. A good net shot can be played by anyone—strength and height are not factors. Touch, deception, and quickness are the best qualities to have.

Underhand Strokes

Underhand strokes are, like the serve, those in which the contact point and the entire head of the racket are below the level of the hand. Those described previously in chapters 2 and 3 are the serve, the hairpin net shot, and the drive. See figure 2.4. The outstanding characteristic of the aforementioned shots and those to be described here, the underhand clear and the underhand dropshot, is that the contact point below net level necessitates an upward stroke.

Underhand Clear   Many of the same stroke production fundamentals of the high, deep, singles serve—the grip, the footwork, the wrist and arm power, and the follow-through—can be applied to the underhand clear. When stroking this clear, the racket swings down from the ready position, under the shuttle for contact, and up, following through in the intended direction of the shuttle. Except for the fact that it originates near the net, the flight pattern the shuttle makes mimics the high, deep serve. Note figure 2.4.

Just as with the overhead defensive clear, the underhand clear is used to gain time to recover the center position and to force the opponent to the backcourt. Its values are many in both singles and doubles. For example, if a dropshot is not particularly good and does not fall close to the net, a large choice of shots is available. But near perfect dropshots necessitate a return with an underhand clear and the stroke becomes indispensable. The only alternative as a return of the perfect dropshot is the hairpin net shot.

Underhand Dropshot   The underhand dropshot described here is played from an area between the short service line and the baseline to the opponent's side of the net and as near to the net as possible. It has specific use both in singles and doubles. Closely related, and yet different in its usage, is the dropshot played closer to the net, the previously described hairpin net shot. See figure 2.5.

Which strokes can you make from A, B, C, D, E?

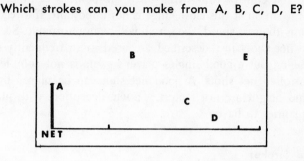

The fundamentals of stroking and the characteristics of the underhand dropshot are almost identical with those of the low serve described in chapter 2. A slow, controlled shot, it has its limitations for this very reason. If it is played from the baseline at a slow pace, your opponent has time to pounce on it at the net. Unless it is disguised by "holding the shuttle" ineffective returns result. Although rarely played successfully from the baseline, its values are exceptional in doubles and mixed doubles when played from midcourt. In doubles, when employed to run the net player from side to side or to draw a player up when both partners are back, panic results. In singles, it can be a superb return of a smash. Directed crosscourt away from the smasher, it forces him to recover quickly and to run the long distance.

Holding the Shuttle

The objective of all underhand shots, other than the serve, is to distract the opponent with deceptive moves. A phrase used often by badminton players, "holding the shuttle," refers to pretending to hit the shuttle before you actually do. For example, if when you pretend to play a dropshot, your opponent moves toward the net and you then flick the shuttle to the backcourt, you have "held the shot." This type of deception is generally employed with underhand shots. Deception on overhead shots results from preparing to stroke each shot identically as described in chapter 2. You may hold the shot by a feint of the racket, head, or body. It takes time, however, to be deceptive. If you are running at full speed to return the shuttle, there is not time to produce feints! When you find the pace is slower and you have the time, reach forward to play the shuttle; then let it drop and contact it at a lower point. During the time the shuttle is dropping, your opponent may be committing himself forward or back. Be alert to this and either drop or flick the shuttle accordingly. If your opponent is moving too soon and getting caught repeatedly, he will be forced to hold his position until you actually contact the shuttle. Continue to watch the shuttle closely. You will tend to take your eye off the shuttle in order to see if and in which direction your opponent is moving. If your errors tell you that you are mis-hitting and indulging in needless fancy racket work, go back to the basics. If you can master this deception, however, it is a tremendous weapon against a player who is very fleet of foot and likes to play a fast game. Slow the game down with defensive shots and then put your deception to work. Hopefully he will tire as a result; then you can apply your pace and power attack.

Using the strokes described in chapters 2 and 3 in an appropriate sequence, you must outthink your opponent. Preconceived strategy and play are fine until you meet your equal or your supposed superior, in which case your thinking must be spontaneous. Your shots must have speed and control, and the decision as to the pattern or order they take must be made in the fury of the game. In singles, perhaps it will be two clears and then the drop, or clear and drop, and drop again; in doubles, a push shot, a smash, and another smash. In either game catch your opponent going the wrong way by not playing to the obvious open space; because he has moved to that obvious space, play behind him. Sometimes you may be caught in your own trap, but if your percentage of "catching" is greater than your percentage of being "caught," then you are ahead of the game. If your strokes are well executed and the rallies are long and the play interesting and close, then consider your game successful. That's the fun of the game. Mastery of the strokes will make it possible for you to delight in meeting a contemporary and pitting your forces against his. Play with enthusiasm and enjoyment. The winning and the rewards, whatever they may be, will be forthcoming. Reaching this stage of enjoyment comes as a result of concentrated practice. No amount of reading and thought off the court can substitute for hours of practice on the court. Both methods of learning, however, must be employed; therefore, the essentials of practicing will be discussed in the next chapter.

Progress
can be speeded up

4

The first step in learning badminton, understanding the why and how of stroke development, must be followed by actual stroke practice. No amount of intellectual grasp of the game can substitute for either repetitive practice of the stroke pattern or coordination of the racket and shuttle to assure correct timing. Mental and physical processes should work together to speed up progress.

DRILLS AND SUGGESTIONS

Various drills and suggestions for the individual will be given in this chapter; group organization will be left to your instructor. In the diagrams that follow, — — — — — — indicates path of the player. For successfully executed drills, locate another student with approximately the same degree of skill; neither player benefits sufficiently if the range of skill varies too greatly.

Overhead Clear Drill (fig. 4.1)

Both players take their center positions where the drill for the clear starts with a singles serve and thereafter continues with clears only. The clears should first be played parallel to the sideline, then crosscourt, then alternating straight and crosscourt, giving each player a chance to clear from both deep corners. The shuttle should be directed repeatedly to the same corner before changing the direction to the other corner. The player stroking from the backhand should be using an overhead or round-the-head clear. The object is to repeatedly clear the shuttle high and deep from one corner to an opposite corner between the doubles and singles back boundary line. Returning to center position after each hit develops good footwork and stamina.

HINT: Get behind and in line with the shuttle for increased depth. Upon contact, step and move your weight towards the net.

Serve Drill

Perfecting the serve, which is one of the easiest strokes to practice, can be done with or without a partner. To permit the server to take his service position for twenty strokes before retrieving shuttles, about twenty shuttles should be collected. This not only saves time but also adds to the consistency of the stroke. The serve, whether for singles or doubles, should be directed to a particular corner on the court. Practice to all corners for singles and doubles. Even if a partner is present, the serve should not be returned; instead, it should be allowed to fall to the court, enabling the server to see exactly how close to the target the shuttle came.

HINT: Drop the shuttle well away from you in order to get the freedom of movement which will result in better accuracy.

Overhead Dropshot and Underhand Clear Drill (fig. 4.2)

Both players begin in the center position from which the drill starts with a singles serve by A to a back corner. The receiver B returns it with an overhead dropshot to a front corner. An underhand clear to the same

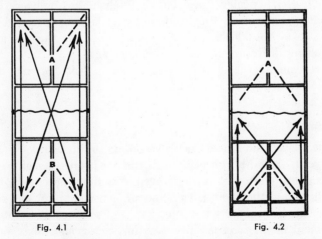

Fig. 4.1

Fig. 4.2

Fig. 4.1 Overhead Clear Drill; Fig. 4.2 Overhead Dropshot and Underhand Clear Drill.

back corner follows·and the drill continues: drop, clear, drop, clear; until one player fails to return the shuttle. The shuttle should be directed repeatedly to the same corner until there is some degree of control before switching the direction of the shuttle to another front or back corner. Again, both players should return to the center position if the drill is to simulate game conditions.

HINT: Pretend to stroke an overhead clear and a hairpin net shot in order to acquire the deception needed for these two shots.

Smash and Underhand Clear Drill (fig. 4.3)

This drill, very much like the preceding drop and clear drill, begins with a singles serve by A to either back corner. The smash by B parallel to the sideline and to the opposite midcourt is returned with a high underhand clear. The drill then becomes—smash, clear, smash, clear; until either player misses; the drill then begins again from center with the serve.

HINT: Gradually increase the speed of your smash in order to eliminate faulty shots.

Drive Drill (fig. 4.4)

There are four drives to be practiced: the straight (parallel to the sideline) forehand and backhand, and the crosscourt forehand and backhand. This drill begins with both players in the center of the court. One player hits a driven serve to the predetermined forehand or backhand of the opponent. Thereafter, repeated drives ensue: forehand to forehand; backhand to backhand; forehand to backhand; and backhand to forehand. Each of the four strokes should be practiced repeatedly before the side and direction are changed. Return to center after each hit.

HINT: Contact the drive high so that this drill does not become a smash, clear drill.

Short Game (fig. 4.5)

This game, played and scored exactly according to singles rules, begins with a low serve by A and return of serve at the net by B: thereafter, only net shots, straight or crosscourt, can be played. Any shots, other than the serve, which fall behind the short service line are considered out of court. This drill, valuable to beginners learning rules and scoring, develops the skill and judgment in the forecourt necessary in doubles and mixed doubles.

HINT: Stand far enough away from the net to give yourself time and space to stroke properly.

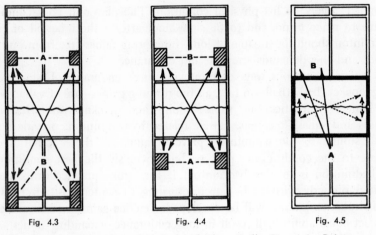

Fig. 4.3   Fig. 4.4   Fig. 4.5

Fig. 4.3   Smash and Underhand Clear Drill; Fig. 4.4   Drive
Drill; Fig. 4.5   Short Game.

Unequal Partner Drill

Many times good players unable to find opponents of like skill can devise
ways of utilizing beginners as practice partners. For instance, the advanced
player strokes the shuttle to one corner of the court to the beginner who
may then return the shuttle any place on the court. The advanced player
develops control by playing the shuttle to the beginner's racket, thus enabling him to keep the rally going. The advanced player develops footwork,
stamina, and stroke control chasing the comparatively uncontrolled returns of the novice. This drill can be amusing and fun to two players de-
siring to learn (each at his own level) and willing to cooperate.

HINT: Enjoy the practice as if it were a game.

Three Stroke Drill

The first three strokes of a point, important because the offense or defense
may easily be determined with initial strokes, should be practiced in that
order and a decision made after each sequence as to the effectiveness of
the serve, return of serve, and the third shot.

HINT: Try to be in an offensive position after the third stroke.

CONDITIONING

Whether a player is able to finish the match or practice period in good
fashion, that is, still stroking the shuttle with power and control, is de-

termined largely by his physical condition. The player in poor condition begins to make errors and to be slow afoot after a short period of time. Badminton should be a game of long, interesting rallies free from outright errors, and this demands strength and endurance.

There are various ways of improving one's endurance. Distance running, hockey, basketball—in fact, all the running games—are of value. Modern dance, gymnastics, and rope skipping add quickness and flexibility. Tennis and squash racquets, closely related to badminton, provide stroke needs similar to the badminton player's game. All these activities contribute to the conditioning process, but obviously the best conditioning for badminton is to play badminton. If the stroke practice drills are rehearsed properly with each player returning to center position between each stroke, endurance will be developed. Practice games against someone of exact equal ability will result in long endurance-demanding rallies.

Needless to say, smoking and alcohol negatively affect one's physical condition. Adequate sleep and food supply the energy needed to meet the demands of a strenuous game.

Skill Games

The games which follow are appropriate for improving various skills for beginners and intermediate players. However, it should be noted that playing these games is not to be considered a substitute for drills. The games may be considered as adjuncts to the drills in that they offer a chance to practice skills developed in drills in a competitive, fun atmosphere.

Quick Score   Procedure:

A game is played and points are won according to the difficulty of the shot. Each team consists of three members. Two members are playing and one member keeps score. The only shot scored is the last shot in the rally. Fifty points constitute a game. Scoring is as follows:

POINTS	SHOT
1	Serve
1	Drop
2	Clear
3	Smash
4	Drive (forehand and backhand)

Number Formation   Procedure:

Each team consists of any number of members. Each member is assigned a number. Members numbered "one" on each of the teams start the

Using drives only, can you and your partner rally the shuttle 4, 6, and then 8 consecutive times?

rally as players. Immediately after one player has hit the shuttle, the caller calls a number. The team member assigned that number on each team immediately moves to take over the rally as a player. The caller must, however, be aware of timing in calling out the number. See following illustration. Points are given to a team each time it makes an error. The first team to reach ten points loses.

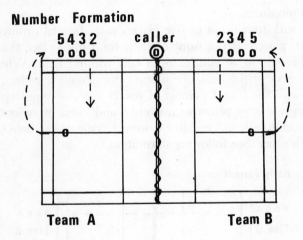

Number Formation

Team A   Team B

CDS   Procedure:
    Play starts with six players on a court (three on each side). Four of the six players are working on the following shots: clear, dropshot, and smash; the other two players are working on net shots. Note the positions of the players on the end lines and at the net.

    Sequence:

    A clears to B, then
    B drops to A, then
    A drops to B, then
    B clears to A, then
    A smashes to B

Both C players are working on net shots. Players rotate as noted in the illustration below.

Formation   **Rotate**

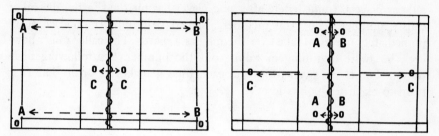

Rally   Procedure:

Begin with four teams of five players each, formed in lines as shown below. Two players at the front of their team lines place the shuttle in play for the purpose of continuing a rally without fault. When a player faults he moves to the back of his team line. Points are given for faults. The team with the fewest number of points in a five-minute period wins. Have students change places with winners and losers of various courts, so that if, for example, line A and line C won the rally, they would be matched against each other. See following illustration.

Rally Formation

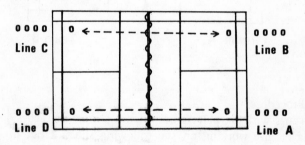

Patterns of play

Certain tactics and strategy apply to all forms of badminton—singles, doubles, or mixed doubles. Tactics are "skillful devices for accomplishing an end," a "mode of procedure for gaining advantage or success." This chapter will discuss the tactics or strategy of badminton.

TACTICS/STRATEGY

Offense and Defense

An important aspect of badminton is the development of offensive and defensive play. Offensive strokes are point winners. They are shots which are directed downward—smashes, half-smashes, dropshots, half-paced drives, and low serves. Winning a point from an overhead position requires speed, sharp angles, and accurate direction. Defensive shots are those hit upward—clear, underhand dropshots, drives, and high serves. Winning a point from an underhand stroke has to be accomplished through deception or superior court positioning.

Offensive and defensive positions may change during the course of a rally. Defense can be changed to offense and vice versa, depending on how well a stroke is executed and selected for use at the proper time. For example, if the smash (offensive) is returned exceptionally well with an underhand hairpin net shot properly angled away from the smasher, and the net shot falls perpendicularly and close to the net, the smasher is forced to hit up (defensive). If, however, the smash had been returned with an underhand clear or weak net shot, the offensive would have remained with the smasher. Offensive players take chances and strive for outright winners whereas defensive players are content to "play it safe" and wait for the opponent to err.

Angle of Return (fig. 5.1)

The angle of return, as important in badminton as it is in tennis, is the angle the returned shuttle takes in relation to the court boundaries. It does not refer to upward or downward angle. Down-the-line and crosscourt shots, with their varying degrees of angle, are commonly used in illustrating angle of return. To avoid being trapped by angle of return, position yourself on the court where the greater percentages of returns are likely to come. Occasionally you can neglect a portion of the court. This is the situation you strive for. For example, a high clear to your opponent's deep forehand (1) or backhand (3) corner can rarely be returned crosscourt high and deep to your diagonal corner because of the long distance. It could be returned with a flat, fast clear towards that corner, but you will be in the center (1 or 3) blocking it before it reaches the intended spot. A shot played to the center of the opponent's court (2) will place the center of the angle of return on the centerline (2). The best plan is to maintain your position in the center of the angle of possible return and then to be alert to the odd shot. Very few players can consistently play the odd shot suc-

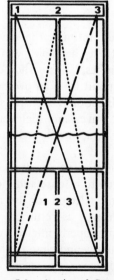

Fig. 5.1   Angle of Return

cessfully. It is generally a question of playing the basic fundamentals better than your opponent and understanding and applying strategic principles.

Crosscourt Shots

Crosscourting and angle of return are closely related. Crosscourt shots travel a long distance across the court, requiring considerable time for the shuttle to arrive at the intended spot. The "down-the-line" shot, a shorter distance, is the more logical shot and yet more obvious. For example, if you play the shuttle to your opponent's forehand side, anticipate the return on your backhand side. Of course, your opponent can crosscourt to your forehand side and must at times, but it will take longer for the shuttle to get there. You therefore will have more time to reach it. Your opponent will crosscourt and play the less desirable shot when he is on balance and can return to center quickly. He will also crosscourt when he discovers you have overanticipated. He too must be on balance when he crosscourts because he has put himself out of the center of his angle of return. A crosscourt shot of any kind played from forehand sideline to forehand sideline leaves the vulnerable backhand sideline exposed. If you decide to stay in the center of the angle and do not deliberately move to cover the down-the-line shots, then these shots become effective, even though obvious. Most of the time you should move about a foot to the side of the court to which you have directed the shuttle. If your shot has pushed your opponent to the back boundary line, you might move one step forward in the hope that he will be unable to get sufficient depth from your good length.

Try to trap him by leading him into overanticipating certain shots because you have played crosscourt or down-the-line shots in a specific pattern. Then play the odd shot for a winner or to draw him away from a particular area. A player generally has a preconceived idea of how much he intends to use crosscourt shots and how to play each opponent. As the game progresses, both players will be trying various plans in hopes of achieving a successful one.

Receiving Serve in Singles (fig. 5.2)

Your ready position for the return of serve for singles and doubles is much the same as the ready position during a rally. Read the description in chapter 2 and note figure 2.3. Variation in the body position is slight. Your feet in this case are placed comfortably apart with the left foot in advance of the right foot in a diagonal stance. This foot position allows an immediate push forward or backward. Serves are usually placed in the front or back corners (short or long) instead of to your side since the service court encompasses only half the width of the entire court. The ability to rush forward to smash the serve or to move back before the high serve gets behind you is imperative. Hence this diagonal stance allows you to reach the shuttle quickly on return of serve. As you take your position to receive the serve, place your feet in the diagonal stance and keep them stationary until the server contacts the shuttle.

In singles most serves are directed high and deep to the corners, and they force the receiver to backpedal quickly in order to get behind the shuttle for an effective return. You should anticipate the usual direction of serves and adjust your waiting position accordingly by shifting your weight to one direction or the other in order to get a faster start. If, however, you overanticipate in either direction, the server is given the opportunity to surprise you completely with a change in direction or depth. Take care to keep your percentages on the return of serve in the proper balance. Note in figure 5.2 that the receiver in the right service court is standing closer to the centerline than to the sideline. This is done to protect his backhand side. In the left service court the receiver moves toward the backhand side for the same purpose. In both cases the receiver is closer to the short service line than to the long service line. This position enables him to attack (hit down) the low serve if it appears. He should have ample time to move back under the high deep serve. A common fault of beginners is to stand too deep in the court, resulting in a defensive (hitting up) return of the low serve.

Since the service court is shorter in doubles than in singles, stand closer to the net so that you can move forward to meet the shuttle at its highest point. See figure 5.5. Just how close you can stand in doubles depends on your ability to move back for the surprise shot. If you are continually ineffectively returning the occasional high serve in doubles, then you will have to relinquish your forward post until your percentage of returns is satisfactory.

Whether you are playing singles or doubles, the general rule to follow is to change your position if you are encountering difficulties. Find the place on the court and the position which best suits you and best defies your opponent's plans.

Singles Strategy

Singles can be described as a "running" game since it requires excellent physical condition to cover the 17 x 44 ft. area. Singles can be a difficult game for some players because it can expose weaknesses that might otherwise be covered up by a partner in doubles play.

The shots utilized most effectively in singles play are the high, deep serve, the overhead clear, the overhead dropshot, the half-smash, the under-

Can you make your opponent move alternately forward and backward five times in succession to receive your hits?
Seven times? Nine times?

---

hand clear, and the hairpin net return. Occasionally a low serve, a driven serve, a drive, a push shot, or a full smash come into use, but these shots are held in reserve primarily for doubles encounters.

In singles, the point generally begins with the basic high serve. The low serve, occasionally used as a change of pace and to throw the receiver off balance, is a method of gaining the offensive since it may descend as soon as it reaches the top of the net and therefore cannot be smashed downward. See figure 2.4 in chapter 2. The more valuable high, deep serve moves the opponent to the back boundary line to enable him to return it; a low serve, returned quickly, gives the server less time and permits the receiver to remain in the center position.

A clear to the opposite backline is the best and safest return of a long high serve. If the high serve falls short of even the doubles back boundary line, then a variety of returns can be played. A dropshot, a smash, a half-smash, or an attacking clear can be employed to gain the offensive; the choice depends on which one you can execute most successfully. This same theory holds true during the rally: shots of poor length can be dealt with more easily and with more variety than can serves or clears that fall perpendicularly on the back boundary line.

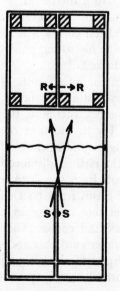

Fig. 5.2   Receiving Serve in Singles

Where should player F position himself to best cover the angle of return for shots directed to A, B, C, D, E?

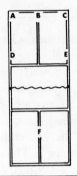

The general plan of attack in singles is to force the opponent to play a backhand from deep in the court. Most players, however, realize the vulnerability of this corner and conjure various defenses for it. The two most common defenses are using the round-the-head shot and moving the center position to the left. Consequently it is often better to open the attack to the forehand side, forcing the player away from the backhand. A fast drive or attacking clear gets the shuttle to the corner quickly. Then you are sure to force your opponent to reply with a backhand rather than a round-the-head or an overhead stroke. The less time he has to play this backhand return the better.

Occasionally the weak area (backhand) is well defended and the strong forehand corner is neglected. In this case, a player's weakness may have become his strong point and his strength may have some flaws that can be attacked.

When the opportunity arises for your opponent to smash or play a dropshot, you must defend as well as possible. Midcourt shots have little value in singles; therefore, the return must be close to the net or on the backline. Try to use your opponent's speed or angle to your advantage by blocking or guiding the shuttle just over the net with a hairpin net shot. Direct it the farthest distance from the stroker. For example, if he smashes or dropshots from the deep forehand corner, then your hairpin net shot should be to his front backhand corner. If your opponent anticipates the hairpin net shot and comes racing in toward the net, then flick a clear to his backhand corner. The next time this situation, the return of the offensive downward shot, occurs, go ahead and play the net shot. Alternate your pattern so that your opponent doesn't know what return to expect or just where to expect it.

Some singles players like the play to be as fast and quick as doubles, whereas others prefer to play a more deliberate power game. The shots characteristic of the quick player are the low serve, the driven serve, the flat clear, the drive, and the smash. The player who needs more time prefers to play the high serve, the high clear, the dropshot, and the half-smash. Many players are adept at both fashions of play and the use of a particular one depends on both the opponent and the situation at hand.

Doubles Strategy

Doubles play, the most popular form of badminton, requires skill, wit, and cleverness. It is exciting, extremely fast, and demands excellent teamwork. It also requires less stamina than singles and is a game in which a weakness in a player's game can be disguised. The low serve, the driven serve, the drive, the half-smash, the smash, and the various net returns are all used effectively in doubles. Through various maneuvers by the two partners, a player may not have to use his less adequate stroke. Instead, both players combine their best assets. Partners unequal in ability can work out a combination that is unusually stable and effective. Four players, all of different skill levels, can combine and have great fun playing.

Three systems of doubles play are used most often. They are side-by-side, up-and-back, and a combination of these two. Men's and ladies' doubles teams use the side-by-side, up-and-back and combination systems; mixed doubles' teams prefer the up-and-back formation.

Side-by-Side or *Defensive Formation* (*Fig. 5.4*)   A team in a sides formation (S and S) divides the court down the middle from net to back boundary line. Each player covers his half of the court, front and back. The basic serving and receiving positions for the sides team place each player in the middle of his half of the court. These positions, alterable as the situation changes, are defensive positions. The "down the middle" shots, those shots directed between the two players, are usually played by the player on the left side since it is his forehand side. A team with a left-handed player will discover some interesting advantages and disadvantages in its system of doubles play that will require some sorting out. It could be agreed that the stronger player is to play the middle shots regardless of which is his forehand side.

The advantage in using the "sides" system is that each player's area to defend is well defined and there is little confusion as to which player is to "cover" which shots. This defensive "sides" formation is the best system when you have been forced to hit the shuttle upward giving your opponents the opportunity to smash. With both players back from the net, they have more time to defend against the smash and to cover the areas (midcourt and backcourt) where a smash can be directed. The disadvantage of the system is that the opposing team can play all the shots to one side, up and back, and tire one player. If one player is weaker than the other, the opponents will naturally launch their attack on him.

Up-and-Back or Offensive Formation (fig. 5.4)   In this system the court is divided in such a way that when a team is on the attack, one player plays the forecourt (U) and the other player (B) plays the backcourt. Note the serving (S) and receiving (R & R) positions for this formation in figure 5.5. The dividing line is about midcourt, depending upon the agreement made by the two partners (P).

The advantage of the up-and-back system lies in the fact that there is always a player at the net to "put away" any loose returns; this keeps the pressure on the opponents. For example, as soon as one player can smash or dropshot from the backcourt, his partner moves forward to the net position to cut off any weak returns. Crosscourt shots can be more easily blocked with a player at the net. In addition, this formation makes it easier (1) to protect weaknesses, and (2) for each player to cover the part of the court to which his game is best suited.

The weakness of the up-and-back system lies in the midcourt area along the sidelines. The shot that is played just behind the net player and just in front of the backcourt player tends to cause confusion as to which player is to hit the shuttle. The resulting slight delay may prove disastrous.

Combination   The combination system is a means of rotating from up-and-back to side-by-side depending on whether a team is defending or attacking. The aggressive team will have to relinquish the up-and-back formation when either player is forced to hit the shuttle upward (defensive); therefore, when on defense, this team reverts to the side-by-side formation until it can regain the attack. The up-and-back formation is an inadequate defense against the smash because the player at net will not have time to defend, and his partner cannot protect the entire backcourt against a smash. The net player backpedals quickly to either side, preferably the closer, and his partner adjusts accordingly.

Serves   Whatever the system used, the serve is highly important as it gives the opportunity to score. In doubles the low, the driven, and the flick serves are used mostly—the low serve being the best. It should be played low to the net, falling at a downward angle after passing the net. Most of the time it should be directed to the inside corner of the service court in order to give your opponent less angle. If the receiver is rushing the serve effectively, the driven and flick serves should be used to dis-

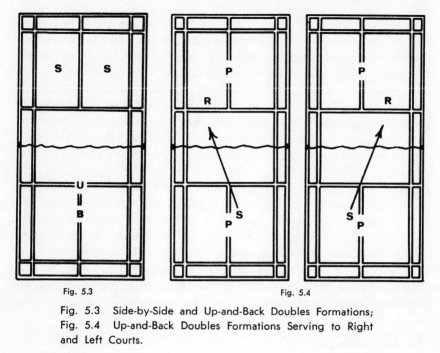

Fig. 5.3

Fig. 5.4

Fig. 5.3   Side-by-Side and Up-and-Back Doubles Formations;
Fig. 5.4   Up-and-Back Doubles Formations Serving to Right
and Left Courts.

courage him from attacking your low serve. Unless the driven and flick
serves surprise him however, he will be able to hit down effectively and
gain the attack. Remember, a serve hitting the top of the net and going
into the correct court is good.

Return of Serve   Any high serve should be returned with a smash or
overhead dropshot, preferably the smash. However, most of the time the
receiver will be low served and has a choice of returning with a drop, drive,
or halfcourt. The *drop* should be deceptive, low, and played straight, not
crosscourted. The *drive* return is used mostly and ideally has a flat trajectory, and when possible, it is directed to the backhand side although
the direction should be varied when necessary. The *halfcourt* is the most
difficult to execute as it has to be almost perfect like the drop return or
it backfires. It should fall behind the net player at a downward angle in
order to force the back player to hit up.

Offense   The primary object of the serve, return of serve, and succeeding shots is to force your opponents to hit up thereby giving your side
the attack. When this objective is reached, the smash, the half-smash and
overhead dropshot come into play. The smash should win the point out-

right or force a weak return for the net man to "put away." When smash-ing, it is very important to be on balance and for the smash to have a sharp downward angle. It should be played to the inside of the opponent who is straight ahead of you. Crosscourt smash only for variety and to keep both opponents alert. The half-smash is extremely useful to change the pace particularly after full paced smashes have been used. Overhead drop-shots will take less effort and therefore they have their merits. Indiscrimi-nate and nonpurposeful smashing is not intelligent. Mix the overhead drop, smash, and half-smash judiciously and the rewards will be obvious.

Defense   Despite all efforts to keep the shuttle going down to maintain the offense, at times your opponents will force you to defend. How good or how bad your opponents are will determine the amount of time you spend defending your court! The smash and dropshot can be returned with a high deep clear, or if possible and ideally with a flatter shot at head or shoulder level. The high deep clear keeps you on defense only with the hope of an error by the smasher. The half-clear or drive return initiates the turn from defense to offense.

Mixed Doubles Strategy

Mixed doubles, played by men and women in the up-and-back formation, is a great attacking game and probably the one played most often at the club or in the backyard. It is superior to many games involving men and women because it is impossible for the man to concentrate his attack on the opposing woman with any degree of success. A more well-balanced game results in badminton than in tennis because the badminton net is at a five foot height and the court is relatively small. For example, if the opposing man decides to smash the shuttle at the woman, she merely ducks below net level and lets the shuttle pass on for her partner to play. Because the court is not very wide, the man can cover it effectively.

See figures 5.6 and 5.7 for serving and receiving positions in mixed doubles. The woman plays the shuttles in the front part of the court cov-ering the short service line to the net. She should let clears, fast drives, and smashes pass her to be played by her partner who is responsible for most shots that arrive behind the short service line. The woman's ob-jective in the mixed doubles combination is to control the attack by keep-ing the shuttle directed downward. This she does by using halfcourt and net shots. Such returns force the opponents to hit the shuttle up allow-ing her partner to smash. She will, of course, "put away" any "loose" (high and short) shots around the net. It is a rare occasion when the woman moves to the backcourt, and when she does it usually leads to confusion

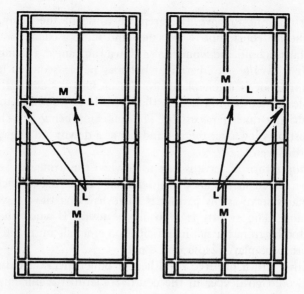

Fig. 5.5 Mixed Doubles Formation—Lady Serving

and loss of pattern play. The man's objective is to play the returns from the backcourt with fast, deceptive strokes which will force weak returns that can be severely dealt with (smashed) by his partner or by himself.

The low serve, always used more offensively in the up-and-back formation than the high serve, must be controlled with great care to keep the receiver from "rushing" the serve; that is, from pushing it quickly to midcourt or smashing it. The low serve should be used most of the time. It may be directed to either corner or to the middle of the service court and close to the short service line. The *ideal* place is to the inside corner, as it narrows the angle of return. A low serve directed to the outside corner may be useful to a receiver who is overanticipating the low inside serve. However, a serve to the alley makes it very difficult on the serving side's man, as the wide angle makes it hard for him to cover the entire backcourt. The flick serve helps keep the receiver from consistently rushing the low serve. Upon occasion a high serve may be delivered to the opposing woman if she has a weak overhead and does not backpedal efficiently.

The return of serve must be varied to keep the opponents from anticipating the return. Any shot or play can be a chance if overused. Returning a serve with a clear is disasterous and not recommended. The serve is most commonly returned with a halfcourt, dropshot, or drive. The choice of which one to use varies; it depends on whether played by the man or the woman, on their abilities, and on the abilities of their opponents. It is difficult to have a set reply because of the many variables. However, the *halfcourt shot* is the safest and most used. It has moderate speed and falls behind the woman at a downward angle, forcing the man to hit up. It is usually played straight but may be crosscourted for variety. The halfcourt shot is often played to the backhand side of the woman as she has less reach behind her on that side. It can be used to slow the pace of a driving duel if necessary. The halfcourt being slower than the drive, it must pass low over the net and fall at a downward angle, or it will be dealt with severely.

The *drop* return of serve is best used when the woman is serving and it should be placed in the alley farthest from her. It is extremely risky to drop the man's serve as his partner is there hawking the net waiting for anything short. The only time it would be useful is when the woman's position is too far from the net in anticipation of a halfcourt, and even then the drop has to be played close to the net.

The *drive* return of serve is pushed or punched faster than the halfcourt and would go deeper in the court. Sometimes a punch directly at the man cramps him and narrows his angle of return as well.

Generally, the drop and halfcourt used judiciously keep the opposing woman in trouble and the drive and halfcourt played successfully keep the opposing man off balance. After the serve and return, and during play, the

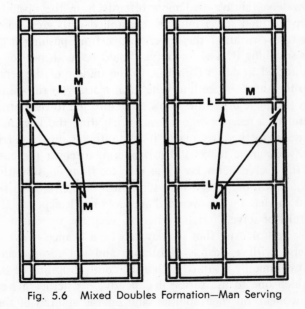

Fig. 5.6   Mixed Doubles Formation—Man Serving

Can you and your opponent playing in "back" position rally the shuttle four times in succession, keeping it out of the reach of your partners as they play in "up" position?

Six times? Ten times?

---

halfcourt and *drive* shots are used most. Lifting the shuttle is what you want your opponents to do so you can win the point on a smash. Therefore, you yourself must avoid lifting. The rallies often generate into driving duels between the two men with the better driver winning. If you know your opponent is excellent at driving, then make more use of the halfcourt and perhaps the drop if the woman is less effective than her partner. The man should use good judgment when electing to crosscourt a drive by being cognizant of his center position.

Occasions will arise when you will be forced to hit up and defend against a smash. Usually the woman should back up several feet and defend against the *crosscourt* smash. The man is then responsible for the down-the-line smash and for the dropshot played straight. This net area has now become vulnerable since the woman has backed out and to one side in an effort to return the crosscourt smash.

In conclusion, try to direct the play to your strengths and to your opponent's weaknesses. Try to play to your partner's best abilities, cooperate, discuss your plans, and above all—enjoy the game! Partners do not enjoy each other if they feel they are not getting to play their own or best shots. The man should not let his ego make him responsible for playing shots which can be better played by his lady partner. The lady should try to play shots that will be dealt with by her man's strengths.

The language
and lore of badminton

Modern sports often have peculiar, albeit fascinating sounding terms. Pursuing the origins of the language of individual sports would doubtlessly provide many hours of interesting research.

For example, what explains the "side" of badminton's "side in," "side out," when there are never more than two players on one side of the net? A bit of investigation reveals that in its early years the game was played by sides consisting of at least three players, and usually four or five! Singles and doubles were nonexistent. Instead, a team consisted of several players who served in turn until they were individually eliminated. When all team members had finished serving, thus completing an inning, that group was said to be "side out." Currently the term "service over" is used in the official rules but players continue to say "side out."

Although singles and doubles are the accepted events in competition today, there are still countries, the majority Asian, where the many-sided game is still popular because of a surplus of badminton players, a lack of available courts, and a lust for long rallies which are, of course, prolonged because every inch of the court is covered by someone!

The derivations of the terms presented in the following glossary are equally fascinating, and pursuit of them by the curious student would promise interesting results. Some of them have been more fully described in earlier chapters of this book.

ABA. American Badminton Association. The national governing body in the United States was founded in 1936.

Alley. Extension of the court by 1½ ft. on both sides for doubles play. Referred to by the English as "tramline."

Back Alley. Area between back boundary and long service lines.

Badminton. The game we know today derived its name from the village of Badminton in Gloucestershire. It was here in the early 1860s at the Duke of Beaufort's estate that this new game, which was brought back from India by some Army officers, was first played in England.

Balk. Any deceptive movement which disconcerts an opponent before or during service. Often called a "feint."

Bird. The object with feathers which flies through the air over a badminton court in place of a ball. Parrot and eagle "birds" are popular in Thailand, bluebirds in Denmark. Officially known as shuttlecock. Commonly referred to as shuttle (fig. 1.3).

Block. Placing the racket in front of the shuttle and letting it rebound into the opponent's side of the court. Not a stroke.

Carry. Momentarily holding the shuttle on the racket during the execution of a stroke. Also called a sling or a throw. This is an illegal procedure.

Center or Basic Position. Position in which a player stands in relation to the lines of the court, the net, the opponent, and the shuttle.

Clear. High, deep shot hit to the back boundary line (figs. 2.8 and 2.4).

Combination Doubles Formation. Rotation of the side-by-side and the up-and-back formations (fig. 5.4).

Court. Area of play. The area bounded by the outer lines of play has not always had the same shape, and the dimensions have, therefore, also differed. Although rules and regulations were drawn up as early as 1877 by Colonel H. O. Selby, Royal Engineers, and published in book form in Karachi, West Pakistan (then a part of India), the numerous different interpretations with reference to the size and shape of the court unfortunately delayed the development of the game. In the early part of the century in India the court was actually laid out on a ground about the size of a lawn tennis court, 78 ft. by 36 ft., and up to five persons played on each side (no wonder!). In England this confusion can be traced to the 1860s when the Duke of Beaufort introduced this glorified form of battledore and shuttlecock to his guests. The room in which the game was played had two large doors opening inwards on the side walls. In order to allow nonplaying guests to enter and leave the room without disturbing the game in progress, it was decided to narrow the court considerably at the net, thus originating the "hour-glass" shaped court. Variations of this peculiarly shaped court were maintained for thirty years, and the first three All-England Championships actually took place under these trying conditions. Even in 1911 two English clubs, playing home and away team matches, found themselves playing first on a court 60 ft. by 30 ft., then on one 44 ft. by 20 ft.!

Crosscourt Shots. Shots hit diagonally from one side of the court to the other.

Deception. The art of deceiving or outwitting one's opponent. Accomplished in badminton with deceptive stroking by changing the direction and speed of the shuttle at the last minute.

Double Hit. Hitting the shuttle twice in succession on the same stroke. An illegal procedure.

Drive. A fast and low shot which makes a horizontal flight pattern over the net (figs. 2.14 and 2.16).

Driven Serve. Quickly hit serve having a flat trajectory (fig. 2.4).

Dropshot. Finesse stroke hit with very little speed which falls close to the net on the opponent's side (fig. 2.10). In Malaysia the slowest type of drop is called the Coconut Drop because it falls perpendicularly. Described in this book as the hairpin net shot (fig. 2.4).

Ends of Court. Refers to the physical boundaries of the court on either side of the net.

Fault. Any violation of the rules. Most faults are broadly classified as either serving or receiving faults, or faults occurring "in play."

First Service. Normally used in doubles. Denotes that the player serving retains service.

Flat. The flight of the shuttle with a level horizontal trajectory. Also, the angle of the face of the racket which does not impart spin to the shuttle.

Flick. Speeding up the shuttle with a quick wrist action. Useful in stroking from below the level of the net, thereby surprising an opponent by quickly changing a soft shot into a faster passing shot.

Game. A game unit consists of fifteen points in men's singles and in all doubles games; eleven points constitutes a game in ladies' singles. See "Setting."

Game Bird. Game winning point.

Hairpin Net Shot. Stroke made from below and very close to the net with the shuttle just clearing the net and then dropping sharply downward. Takes its name, hairpin, from the shape of the shuttle's flight in a perfectly executed shot (fig. 2.4).

Halfcourt Shot. Shot placed midcourt. Used more in doubles than in singles play, especially against the up-and-back formation (fig. 2.7).

Hand. An outdated term meaning service. First Hand and Second Hand are now correctly called First Service and Second Service.

IBF. International Badminton Federation. The world governing body established in July, 1934, at which time badminton had become sufficiently worldwide in its appeal to warrant international organization. The IBF is governed by an annual meeting of the elected representatives of every national association included in its membership. One of its many functions is the management of the world famous international team competitions for the Thomas Cup and the Uber Cup.

Inning. Term of service. Time during which a player or side holds the service.

In Play. The shuttle is said to be "in play" from the time it is struck by the server's racket until it touches the ground or a fault or let occurs. See exception in Laws (chap. 7).

"In" Side. Player or team having the right to serve.

Kill. Fast downward shot which usually cannot be returned. A putaway.

Let. Legitimate cessation of play to allow an exchange or rally to be replayed.

Love. No score. English pronunciation of the French word "l'œuf" meaning goose-egg or zero. To start a singles match the umpire calls "Love-All, Play." To start a doubles match he says "Hand Out, Love-All, Play."

Love-All. No score. Also used after a game has been set. See "setting."

Match. Best two out of three games.

Match Point. Match-winning point.

Net Shot. Shot hit from the forecourt with the shuttle just clearing the netcord. Hairpin net shots, push shots, and net smashes are the three most popular net shots (fig. 2.4).

New York Badminton Club. Founded in 1878, the NYBC claims to be the oldest organized club in the world, although until the early part of this century it was more a club of social prominence than a center designed for badminton activity.

No Shot. Badminton etiquette requires a player to immediately call "no shot" when he has faulted by carrying, slinging, or throwing the shuttle.

"Out" Side. Side receiving serve: opposite of "in" side.

Point. Smallest unit in scoring.

Poona. Some historians believe the original name for badminton was "poona," the name coming from the city of Poona in India where a badminton-type game was played in the 1860s.

Push Shot. A gentle net shot played by merely pushing the shuttle without force (fig. 2.4).

Ready Position. An alert body position enabling the player to make quick movement in any direction (fig. 2.3).

Round-the-Head Shot. Stroke peculiar to badminton. An overhead stroke played on the left side of the body. The contact point is above the left shoulder (fig. 3.1).

Rush the Serve. Quick spurt to the net in an attempt to put away a low serve simply by smashing the shuttle down into an opponent's court. Used mostly in doubles.

Second Service. Normally used in doubles. Indicates that one partner is "down," i.e., he has already had his turn at serving.

Serve or Service. Act of putting the shuttle into play. Opening stroke of each exchange or rally (fig. 2.5).

Service Court. Area into which serve must be delivered, determined by the score.

Setting. Method of extending games by increasing the number of points necessary to win tied games. Player reaching tied score first has option of setting. Further described in chapter 7.

Set Up. Poor shot which makes a "kill" easy for the opponent.

Shuttlecock (fig. 1.3). Official name for shuttle or "bird." The traditional shuttlecock, made with precious goose feathers and described in chapter 9, is still used officially in all major competitions today. The first synthetic shuttle was made from plastic. More recently, nylon shuttles represent a considerable improvement over the plastic ones, and are popular in less important tournaments as well as in club matches. Shuttles have varied over the years. Early tournament players often had their choice between a "rocket" and a "slow wobbler." They continued playing with one shuttle until it lost several feathers as well as its original shape. Those used in the first few All-England Championships were called barrel shuttles because of their shape. In early years unsuccessful efforts were made to produce fabric and papier-mache shuttles. India tried making a substitute ball of Berlin wool wound on a double disc of cardboard 2½ in. in diameter with a central hole of 1 in., but it flew too fast.

Side-by-Side. A doubles formation (fig. 5.4).

Side-In and Side-Out. See beginning of this chapter.

Smash. Hard hit overhead shot which forces the shuttle sharply downward. The game's chief attacking stroke (fig. 2.12).

Stroke. Action of striking the shuttle with the racket.

Toss. Before play begins, opponents toss a coin or spin a racket, and the player winning the toss or spin has a choice of serving, receiving, or making a choice of sides.

Up-and-Back. Popular doubles and mixed doubles formation (fig. 5.4).

Wood Shot. The shot which results when the base of the shuttle is hit by the frame of the racket rather than by the strings. Although they have not always been legal, the IBF ruled in 1963 that wood shots were acceptable.

Laws of the game

7

The International Badminton Federation together with the American Badminton Association annually publishes a handbook containing the rules of badminton, officially termed "laws," as well as interpretations and revisions of these laws. Although an official handbook should be consulted for any tournament play, the following set of rules will suffice for scholastic and recreational play. The IBF has established laws pertinent to the court, equipment, players, toss, method of scoring, etc.

Playing Surface and Equipment

1. The singles court measures 17 ft. wide and 44 ft. long; the doubles court measures 20 ft. wide and 44 ft. long. See figures 1.1 and 1.2 in chapter 1.

2. A net 5 ft. 1 in. in height bisects the court; the net posts are placed on the doubles sideline. The net dips in the center to a height of exactly 5 ft.

3. A detailed description of the official present-day shuttle will be found in the section on equipment. In order to insure the game's taking the same form whenever and wherever it is played, it is imperative to standardize a shuttle's speed. A profound difference in the type of game results if a fast shuttle instead of a slow shuttle is selected for use. The heavier the shuttle, the faster it flies. Each grain adds about four inches in length to its flight. The shuttle also flies faster under conditions of increased temperature and altitude. Weights of manu-

factured shuttles therefore vary from 73 to 85 grains in order to meet conditions at a particular time. Under normal conditions a 79- or 80-grain shuttle should be used. Each time the game is played the shuttle should function at the same speed regardless of atmospheric conditions. The testing of a shuttle's speed takes place just before matches are to begin.

The test is made by having a player of average strength strike the shuttle with a full underhand stroke from a spot immediately above the back boundary line in a line parallel to the sidelines and at an upward angle. It is deemed correctly paced if it falls not less than 1 ft. or more than 2 ft. 6 in. short of the other back boundary line (see fig. 7.1).

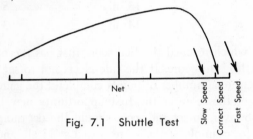

Fig. 7.1   Shuttle Test

Players

4. Players are those persons taking part in the game: one player on a side in singles, two players on a side in doubles. The side which has the serve is called the "in" side and the opposing side, the "out" side.

Toss

5. Before play begins, the opposing sides shall toss a coin or a racket. The winner of the toss shall have the option of serving first, not serving first, or choosing ends of the court. The side losing the toss shall then have a choice of the remaining alternatives. Decisions made at this time can be very important. One end of the court may be more desirable than the other because of lighting arrangements, floor conditions, and location of spectators. Outdoors, the wind and sun are major factors.

Scoring

6. Play is started by an underhand serve, and a side can score only when serving (fig. 7.2). Each time an exchange or rally is won while serv-

ing, one point is recorded. If the exchange is lost while serving, neither side is awarded a point. Instead, the right to serve is relinquished and the opposing side then has the chance to serve and score.

7. Doubles and men's singles games consist of 15 points; ladies' singles, 11 points. Peculiar to the scoring system is the term "setting." This is a method of extending the length of a game if the game is tied at a particular score. See the chart below.

POINTS IN GAME	SCORE SET AT	POINTS REQUIRED TO WIN GAME
11	9 all	3 points
11	10 all	2 points
15	13 all	5 points
15	14 all	3 points

The side which reached the tied score first has the option of setting or not setting the score. If the side elects not to set the score, then the conventional number of points completes the game. A side which did not set the score at the first opportunity may have the opportunity, however, to set the score should the occasion arise again. In doubles, for example, if the score is tied at 13 all, and the team that reached 13 first declared no set, then play continues to 15. If, however, the score becomes tied at 14 all, whichever team reached 14 first is offered the opportunity to set the score.

8. A match shall consist of the best of three games. The players change ends at the beginning of the second game and at the beginning of the third game, if a third game is necessary to decide the match. In the third game, players shall change sides when either player first reaches 8 in a game of 15 points and 6 in a game of 11 points. The object of this change of ends is to try to give both players equal time on both ends of the court. If players forget to change ends, they shall change as soon as their mistake is discovered.

9. An inning indicates a term of service and there may be any number of innings since many rallies are played for which no points are scored.

10. In doubles, each player on a team of two players is referred to as a server while serving his inning. First service is when the initial player is serving. Second service is when the other player serves. Service over occurs when both servers lose their serves. The side or team beginning a game has only one turn at serving in its first inning. Thereafter, both players on a side have a turn and both players take their turn in the innings.

Playing the Game

11. If a player attempting a serve misses the shuttle completely, he may restroke. An infinite number of attempts may be made provided the racket does not touch any part of the shuttle.

12. A serve is deemed completed as soon as the shuttle is struck by the server's racket. Unlike the serve in tennis, only one serve is allowed a player to put the shuttle into play.

13. After the serve is completed, players on both sides may take any positions they wish irrespective of boundaries.

14. A shot falling inside the boundaries or directly on a line is considered good.

15. In singles, players serve from and receive in the right service court when the server's score is zero or an even number. When the server's score is an odd number of points, players serve from and receive in the left service court.

16. In doubles, when their score is an even number, partners should be in the courts (right or left service court) in which they began the game. When the team's score is an odd number, then their court positions should be reversed.

17. The player or team that wins a game always serves first in the next game. At this point, in doubles, a team's serving order may be changed. For example, the losing team might decide that it could be more successful if a different player served first.

18. When any unusual occurrence interferes with the play, a "let" (replay of the point) can be invoked. This happens, for example, if a stray shuttle from a nearby court interferes, or if a linesman and umpire are unable to make a decision on a particular shot.

    The IBF has also some established laws (adopted by the ABA) which cannot be violated without penalty. If any violation of the following laws occur, it is either point or side-out. In other words, if the receiving side errs, the serving side scores a point; if the serving side breaks a rule, no point is scored but it becomes service over and the opponents then serve.

Faults During Serving and Receiving

19. A serve must be an underhand stroke and the shuttle must be contacted below the server's waist. To further insure that the serve is an underhand stroke, the shaft of the racket must point downwards

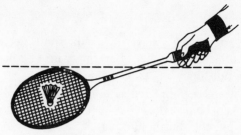

Fig. 7.2   Legal Serve

and the entire head of the racket must be below the hand and fingers holding the racket. See frame 3 of figure 2.5, and figure 7.2.

20. A player's feet must be stationary and in their correct court upon delivery of the serve. It is not a fault if a server takes up his stance and then takes one step forward, provided he has not started to swing his racket before completing the step.

21. The server should not serve until the receiver is ready. If the receiver attempts to return the serve, however, he is judged ready. If a player is not ready, he should let the shuttle fall to the court and then tell the server or the umpire that he was not ready, in which case the serve shall be delivered again. This rule keeps the player who has a tendency to hurry his opponent from gaining an undue advantage.

22. No preliminary feints or movements to distract the receiver before he contacts the shuttle are allowed. A preliminary feint is any movement by the server that has the effect of breaking the continuity of the serve after the two players have taken their ready positions to begin the point. Such action is termed a balk, and a balk is a fault. It is also a fault if the server delays hitting the shuttle for so long as to be unfair to the receiver.

23. A serve that lands outside the boundaries of the service court is a fault.

24. A player may not serve out of turn or from the wrong court, and the receiver may not be in the wrong court. The consequences of an infraction of this rule depend upon when the mistake is discovered. If the player who commits one of these serving or receiving errors wins the rally, and the mistake is then discovered, a let is called. If the player at fault loses the rally, the mistake stands, that is, no let. If the mistake is not discovered before the next point commences, the already altered serving and receiving order is not changed until the end of the game regardless of which team won or lost the rally.

25. A serve may not be received twice in succession in an inning by the same player in doubles. If this occurs and points are scored, the error stands and the next serve is delivered to the other player.

26. The receiver's partner may not strike a serve meant for his partner.

27. If the shuttle falls outside the boundaries, passes through or under the net, fails to pass the net, touches the roof or side walls, or touches a person or the dress of a person, the rally ceases and the player committing the fault is penalized. However, a serve hitting the top of the net and going into the correct service court is legal and "in play." Some gymnasiums or halls may have low beams, ropes, or other obstructions hanging over the court. In such cases the local association may establish a ground rule to the effect that a shuttle hitting the obstruction would not be considered a fault, but a let. If careful judgment by an experienced person is not made in this case, a player might intentionally hit the obstruction when it appeared that he was going to lose the point. If an obstruction can be hit deliberately, the fault rule is usually enforced. An unusual and uncommon situation develops when a shuttle passes the net outside of the net post and then flies into the court. This is the only case in which the shuttle can go below the net level and still be legal. It is most likely to occur outside on a windy day.

28. A player may not reach over the net to contact a shuttle. He may, however, contact the shuttle on his side of the net and follow through with his racket on the opponent's side, providing the net is not touched.

29. When the shuttle is "in play" a player may not touch the net or the net posts with his body, his racket, or his clothing. If he should hit the net following a stroke and after his shot has struck the floor, a fault does not result because the shuttle is not "in play" after it strikes the floor.

30. The shuttle may not be hit twice in succession before being returned to the opponent. This rule prevents setting the shuttle up to oneself or to one's partner.

31. The shuttle may not rest momentarily on the racket during the execution of the stroke. Commonly called "carry," "sling," or "throw," it is difficult to detect this fault, and it is often committed unintentionally by beginners because of poor timing. More advanced players seldom commit this fault outright, but occasionally when a deceptive technique is attempted the infraction may occur. When a "carry" is committed, the shuttle's speed and direction are changed. This naturally handicaps the receiver of such a shot, and a player should

not be penalized by another's player's poor technique. The rule, then, is an essential one, and any player at fault should immediately call "No Shot."

32. A fault is called when a player is hit by the shuttle whether he is standing inside or outside the court boundaries. It is surprising to many players to realize that if they are able to hit their opponent with the shuttle, the point is theirs! This, however, is more difficult to accomplish than it sounds.

33. If a shuttle is hit into the net or caught in the net on the striker's side, it is not "in play." If the shuttle goes over the net, a let results. The point is replayed since the player on whose side the shuttle was caught did not have a fair chance of returning the shuttle. If the player attempted to play the shuttle that was caught in the net and in doing so hit the net, then a "fault," rather than a let, would be called.

34. A player may not step on his opponent's side of the net even when, in returning a close net shot, he cannot stop his momentum until his feet are in his opponent's court.

35. A player may not bend down below the net and intentionally hold his racket above the net hoping that the shuttle will happen to rebound from his racket into the opponent's court. This occasionally happens when a player close to the net tries to defend against a smash. On the other hand, a racket held in front of a player's face for protection is a good maneuver and any resulting shot is acceptable.

36. A player may not "unsight" another player. This rule, applicable only in doubles, means that the server's partner cannot stand in front of the server in such a way that the receiver cannot see the shuttle about to be served. If this situation occurs, the receiver tells the server or the umpire, before the shuttle is served, that he cannot see the shuttle. An adjustment of the starting positions is then made by the serving side.

Disqualification

37. Play must be continuous. A player violating this rule is not just faulted, he is disqualified. A player therefore may not leave the court, receive advice, or rest at any time from the start to the conclusion of the match. The umpire shall judge whether this rule has been broken and shall disqualify any offenders. Certain countries, where

climatic conditions make it desirable, allow a five-minute rest period between the second and third games.

A thorough and accurate knowledge of the rules makes for a smooth, pleasurable game. Many misunderstandings can be avoided by the player who knows not only the rules but the reasons for them.

Unwritten rules

Badminton, like all sports, has unwritten as well as written rules. The etiquette of badminton, which is basically consideration for other people, commences with your first introduction to the game.

First of all, attractive attire contributes to a wholesome atmosphere. Clean, white, comfortable clothing has always been the standard dress for racket sports and this unwritten rule should be adhered to regardless of a player's skill.

Certain standards should be followed when a club is organized in the neighborhood or at school. Members should be prompt in paying dues, attend meetings regularly, and assist in putting up and taking down the nets. Because of their expense, shuttles can present problems. Occasionally, club dues pay for their purchase and the person in charge of this detail must work out a system which is fair to everyone, for their use. Usually, however, each player brings his own shuttles to club gatherings. In this case each player should contribute two or three new shuttles for the evening's play. If two players decide to practice at times other than regular club meetings, both players must make sure they arrive with plenty of good shuttles. In every club there are one or two players who always appear without shuttles or with some of inferior quality. This type of person finds he is not invited to play in certain groups and often wonders why! If guests are invited to your court or club to play, the hosts should furnish all the shuttles.

During informal or competitive play, a player's personality may be disclosed, sometimes quite obviously, sometimes not. The quickness of the game brings out responses that are spontaneous, reflecting the character of the player. For example, a fault shot (carry, throw, sling) must be called before the opponent attempts a return. The player delaying the call "no shot" confuses the other players and the ensuing play. Another unacceptable way to make decisions—pretending not to know whether the shot was a fault—forces someone else to make a decision that is not his responsibility. The habit of continually suggesting that points be replayed when a player cannot make a particularly close decision is especially irritating. If, for example, every time a player places a shuttle on or near a line the opponent cannot make a decision as to whether it is in or out, even those shots that are well placed are nullified. Obviously this is discouraging to the accomplished player. Unsporting players who deceive themselves into thinking others are not aware of these finer points of etiquette establish unenvied reputations.

In informal play, the server usually takes the responsibility of calling the score after each rally. This eliminates many unpleasant discussions. Both players should keep the score to themselves even though they may not be responsible for calling it aloud. Keeping the score is valuable, of course, in planning the strategy for the next point.

In mixed doubles the man can demonstrate good manners in many ways. The lady usually serves first, crosses the net first when changing sides, and is consulted when any decisions are to be made. If conventional politeness is displayed between men and women both on and off the badminton court, no obvious display of manners is necessary.

Needless to say, emotional outbursts such as racket throwing and abusive language have no place in badminton and the customary absence of this type of behavior makes the game attractive to players and spectators alike. Even in the most highly competitive areas the sportsmanship is superior, perhaps even more so at this level. The champion must be a good example to others, particularly to youngsters, who emulate the winner in every way.

Some unwritten etiquette procedures apply specifically to the tournament player, but beginners and club players may find them useful also. When entering a tournament, the player should fill out his entry accurately, supplying all the information requested. This is a distinct advantage to the tournament committee responsible for making the draw, scheduling the matches, housing the players, and publicizing the tournament. The entry blank should be returned no later than the date requested. Players should not expect tournaments to accept late entries and should not protest when they are not accepted. Upon arriving at the scene of the tournament, the entrant should report immediately to the committee in charge in order to determine the time and court number for his match. The default time of fifteen minutes should not be extended by the player at any time.

A player should find out who he is to play and should introduce himself to his opponent if they have not previously met. A friendly attitude should prevail between opponents from the start until the conclusion of their association.

Prior to the warm-up period, a shuttle suitable to both players should be tested and selected. During the warm-up time, the shuttle should be kept in play in order to give the opponent a fair chance to move around and hit the shuttle a sufficient number of times. Be sure your opponent is ready before you serve to him and be ready yourself when he is ready to serve. Retrieve shuttles that fall in your court and those on your opponent's side by the net if you are closer. Return the shuttle directly to the server, not just anywhere in his court. If a shuttle becomes damaged during play, it is courteous to ask your opponent if a change of shuttle can be made. An occasional compliment, "fine shot," on your opponent's winning stroke has always been acceptable! Maintain a spirit of fairness and generally it will be reciprocated. In addition, play your best; careless play is an insult to your opponent.

Following the completion of a match a player should always shake hands and, depending upon the outcome of the match, either congratulate his opponent on winning or thank him for playing the match. He should always thank the umpire too, and then report the score to the official table and inquire as to the time of his next match.

Learn to win and lose gracefully. It is unnecessary to expound on your victories; any good play will be noticed. A defeat should not be blamed on a minor or trivial matter, nor should excuses be found for poor play. Instead keep your thoughts to yourself, analyze the match, and determine to do better the next time.

The final obligation of a gracious tournament player is to write thank-you notes to the tournament or school officials and to the people who have shown special courtesies such as supplying housing and meals. This detail must be attended to promptly and is equal in importance to the sending in of the original entry.

Facts for enthusiasts

EQUIPMENT FOR BADMINTON

A racket, a shuttle, and a court with a net are all that are really needed to play badminton. Fortunately, this equipment is readily available and relatively inexpensive. Complete sets which include all the necessary equipment are available in most sporting goods stores, or each item can be purchased separately. Since a racket is the most important item of equipment, novices should ask an experienced person to help in its selection. Try several rackets, finally choosing the one which has the correct balance and a grip that feels comfortable. No rules or specifications govern the size of the racket. It may be any length or weight a player desires. Manufacturers have, however, arrived at a standard size which is 26 in. in overall length; approximately 10 in. is in the head, 11 in. in the shaft, and 5 in. in the grip. The balance point is the midpoint or 13 in. from either end. Rackets weigh from $4\frac{1}{2}$ to $5\frac{1}{2}$ ounces.

Until recently rackets were made entirely of wood, but now those of quality are usually constructed of hickory wood with a steel or fiberglass shaft. In recent years, many players have been using the lighter weight metal racket strung with nylon. The metal rackets can be strung more tightly with nylon than with gut. Also, there is no need for a press since the metal does not warp as might the wooden frames. However, there is no widespread opinion as to which is better—wood or metal. It is still a matter of personal preference. A good racket will cost about $18.95 but one entirely suitable for school and recreational play can be purchased for

$6.95. The racket can be strung with lamb's gut or nylon strings. **Tournament** players like rackets tightly strung with good quality gut. A tightly strung racket will "ping" while one strung too loosely will have a "plud" upon contact with the shuttle or when strummed with the fingers. Nylon strings are less expensive than gut and are perfectly adequate for club and school use. This type of string is resistant to moisture and maintains its playing qualities from one season to the next.

To prevent wooden rackets from warping, they should be kept in a press when not in use, while the screws on the press should be so tightened as to exert equal pressure on the racket frame. A laminated racket frame is less apt to warp than one made of a single piece of wood. The tighter a racket is strung the more likely it is to warp. To keep rackets and strings in top condition, they should not be stored in exceptionally damp or dry places.

The selection of a shuttle will depend upon the amount of money available and the objectives of the player. The feathered shuttle used most often in tournament play is the most fragile, the most expensive and requires the most care. It must weigh from 73 to 85 grains and have fourteen to sixteen feathers attached to a kidskin-covered cork base. The feathers should be from 2½ to 2¾ in. in length from the tip of the feathers to the cork base. The feathers should flare at the top from 2⅜ to 2½ in. These specific requirements give the shuttle its unusual, although entirely predictable, flight patterns which are quite different from those of a ball. Synthetic shuttles are manufactured exactly to the foregoing specifications except that the feathers are of nylon and made in one piece. A good synthetic shuttle costs about as much as a feathered shuttle, 85 to 95 cents, but it lasts many times longer.

Proper care of shuttles, particularly the feather ones, is vital to preserving them and extending the length of time they can be used. Feathered shuttles come in tubes with instructions as to the humidity necessary to prevent drying and the resultant breaking of feathers. Any time a feather becomes ruffled, it should be smoothed out. Obviously, any action that would damage or break the feathers should be avoided. Although synthetic shuttles with nylon feathers are more durable, prudence should be shown in storing and handling them too.

Nets and net posts are essential for play. The least expensive net costs about $6.95. The official tournament net is priced at $13.50. The price of net posts ranges from $6.95 to $125.00. The top-priced posts are excellent for club or school use and are light weight aluminum posts with floor plates fixed permanently in the floor.

Current information on badminton may be obtained by writing to the American Badminton Association Executive Secretary, Virginia Lyons, at 1330 Alexandria Drive, San Diego, California 92107.

Jack Van Pragg, 380 S. Euclid Ave., Apt. 207, Pasadena, California 91101, is the news chairman of the ABA and is a source of various information. For information more international in scope, write to the International Badminton Federation, 4 Madeira Avenue, Bromley, Kent, England.

OFFICIATING

The officials needed to conduct a badminton match are as follows: an umpire, one or two service judges, and ten linesmen. At International and World Championships every match has this full complement of officials. In the United States, however, twelve or thirteen officials are rarely available until the final round. Many state and school matches are without any officials whatsoever, in which cases the players themselves keep score and conduct the match. What an opportunity for sportsmanship and fair play, which after all is what badminton is about!

Briefly, the duties of the various officials are as follows. The *Umpire* conducts the match, keeps and calls the score, and enforces the Laws of Badminton. He may be assisted by a *Service Judge* who sees to it that there are no illegal serves (Rules 20 & 22), and no serving faults (Rule 19). If there are two *Service Judges* available, the second one sees to it that the receiver does not commit faults during service (Rule 20). *Linesmen* stationed at various positions adjacent to the court determine whether the shuttlecock is inside or outside the line and the decision of the linesman making the determination is final. If the Service Judges or Linesmen cannot make a decision, they may ask the Umpire to do so. Lack of space here prevents detailed explanation of officiating techniques, but for those particularly interested in this facet of the game, information can be found in the *ABA Rules Book* or *IBF Handbook*. See the following illustration.

TOURNAMENT _INTERCOLLEGIATE CHAMPIONSHIPS_ COLLEGE _ODESSA COLLEGE_

EVENT _MEN'S DOUBLES_ DATE _MARCH 4-6, 1975_

JOE ALSTON
STAN HALES vs _DON PAUP_
JIM POOL

Umpire
Service Judge
Linesmen

		Settings	total
Right	ALSTON	1,2,3,4/ 5,6,7,8,9/ 10,11,12/	12
Left	HALES		
Right	PAUP	1,2,3,4,5,6,7/ 8,9,10,11,12/ 13,14,15	15
Left	POOLE		
Right	ALSTON	1,2,3,4,5/ 6,7,8/ 9,10,11,12/ 13,	14,15,16/ Settings	16
Left	HALES		
Right	PAUP	1,2/ 3,4,5,6,7/ 8,9,10,11/ 12,13/	14,15,16,17,18/	18
Left	POOLE		
Right			total
Left		Settings	
Right			total
Left			

Winner(s) _PAUP - POOLE_ _15-12_ _18-16_

Umpire's Signature _Jack van Paap_

Start Server's Score in space following last score of previous server.

Eg. (a) 1, 2, 3, 4, 5/ 6, 7/ .
(b) 1, 2, 3/ 4/ .

INSTRUCTIONS FOR SCORING:

SINGLES: Place DASH (/) after score when service over. Eg. 1,2,3,4/

DOUBLES: Place DOT (•) above score when first service down.
Place DASH (/) after score when service over. Eg. 1,2,3,4,5,6/

Sample Score Sheet

Playing the game

10

Although badminton is still considered a minor sport in the United States, there is evidence that it is becoming increasingly popular. It is played in backyards, schools, and clubs, and there are numerous levels of competition for all players.

The governing body of the sport in the United States is the American Badminton Association. The ABA governs the six badminton regions of the United States, which in turn administer the activities of the state associations and their member clubs. Any member of an affiliated club automatically becomes a member of the ABA. Clubs usually meet at a school, a YMCA, or at a club especially built for badminton. Any person who wishes to play in a tournament sanctioned by the ABA must belong to a member club or have a direct membership with the ABA. Most tournaments, with the exception of school events, are sanctioned. A list of clubs and their addresses is published in *Badminton USA*, the official publication of the ABA.

Many tournaments (all indoors) are available to the interested amateur competitor. Each region has a tournament sanction chairman who organizes and schedules the events in his region. Information regarding the chairman and the schedules can be found in *Badminton USA*. At present there are club, state, regional, intercollegiate, and national amateur championships. National championships are held for men and women in singles, doubles, and mixed doubles, in the several age-based divisions.

Professionalism in badminton is on a very moderate scale, limited mainly to teaching professionals. A few of the leading players of the world have turned professional and have coached in various countries. There has been a minimum of professional tours, although Hugh Forgie and Shirley Marie have appeared regularly in the Ice Capades.

The International Badminton Federation, founded in 1934, is the organization that governs the sport internationally. It consists of forty-six affiliated national badminton associations, one of which is the ABA, which joined in 1938. Thirty-one years before the IBF came into being, the first mixed team match took place between England and Ireland. Since that time more than thirty-five countries around the world have participated in similar matches. Denmark, England, Indonesia, the United States, West Germany, and Malaysia are the most active international participants.

The All-England Championships is the oldest and most famous badminton tournament in the world, and it always attracts entries from many countries. It was first held in 1899, and has grown in strength and importance almost every year since. Play now is consistently witnessed by thousands.

The Swiss Badminton Federation instituted the Helvetia Cup in 1961-62; it provides team matches among Austria, Belgium, France, Netherlands, West Germany, and Switzerland.

The Nordic Championships, started in 1962-63, are individual matches played annually by representatives from Denmark, Finland, Norway, and Sweden. In 1962 badminton was officially introduced into the Asian Games (contests every four years). In August of 1966 the game was introduced into the British Empire and Commonwealth Games at Kingston, Jamaica.

The Thomas Cup is competed for triennially by men from countries that are affiliated with IBF. Sir George Thomas, founder-president of the IBF, donated this renowned trophy for international competition among men's teams. The matches are composed of five singles matches and four doubles matches. To date, Malaysia and Indonesia have dominated the event, Malaysia having won four times. Since first competing in 1957, Indonesia has won the Thomas Cup five times in six attempts, which is a magnificent record.

The Ladies International Badminton Championship for the Uber Cup is also held triennially. The team trophy was donated by one of England's greatest players, Mrs. H. S. (Betty) Uber. The United States has held the cup three times since its inauguration in 1957. The 1968-69 competition for the Cup was held throughout the world, with the challenge round in Tokyo. The Japanese team was the holder and retained the cup at this meeting. The more recent competitions have been won by Indonesian as well as Japanese teams.

Selected references

Books

Breen, James L. *Badminton.* (Sports Techniques Series). Chicago: Athletic Institute (805 Merchandise Mart Plaza), 1970.

Brown, Edward. *The Complete Book of Badminton.* Harrisburg, Pa.: Stackpole Books, 1969.

Choong, Eddy and Brundle, Fred. *Badminton.* New York: Dover Publishing Co., Inc., 1953.

Davidson, Ken and Gustavson, Lea. *Winning Badminton.* New York: Ronald Press, 1964.

Davis, Pat. *Badminton Complete* (American Edition). Cranbury, N. J.: A. S. Barnes & Co., 1967.

Devlin, J. Frank; Lardner, Rex; and the Eds. of Sports Illustrated. *Sports Illustrated Book of Badminton.* rev. ed. New York: J. B. Lippincott Co., 1973.

Hashman, Judy Devlin. *Badminton: A Champion's Way.* London: Kaye & Ward Ltd., 1973.

Hicks, Virginia. *The How To of Badminton from Player to Teacher.* Denton, Tex.: Terrell Wheeler Printing Inc., 1973.

Poole, James. *Badminton.* 2d ed. (Goodyear Physical Activities Series). Pacific Palisades, Calif.: Goodyear Publishing Co., 1969.

Rogers, Wynn. *Advanced Badminton.* (Physical Education Activities Series). Dubuque, Ia.: Wm. C. Brown Company Publishers, 2460 Kerper Blvd., 1970.

Rutledge, Abbie and Friedrich, John. *Beginning Badminton.* Belmont, Calif.: Wadsworth Publishing Co., 1969.

Sullivan, George. *Guide to Badminton.* New York: Fleet Press Corp., 1968.

Magazines and Guides

ABA Handbook. American Badminton Association. 1330 Alexandria Dr., San Diego, Calif. 92107.

Badminton Gazette. Badminton Association of England. 12A, Palmerston Road, Buckhurst Hill, Essex, England.

Badminton Review. Canadian Badminton Association, 333 River Road, Ottawa, Ontario, Canada.

Badminton Technique Charts. DGWS-AAHPER, 1201 16th St., N.W., Washington, D. C. 20036.

Badminton USA. Official Publication of the American Badminton Association, Bea Massmann, 333 Saratoga Rd., Buffalo, N.Y. 14226.

IBF Handbook. International Badminton Federation. H.A.E. Scheele, ed. 4 Madeira Avenue, Bromley, Kent, England.

Ideas for Badminton Instruction. Lifetime Sports Education Project, 1201 Sixteenth St., N.W., Washington, D. C. 20036.

Official Rules. American Badminton Association, Mrs. Virginia Lyon, 1330 Alexandria Dr., San Diego, Calif., 92107.

Selected Tennis & Badminton Articles. DGWS-AAHPER, 1201 16th St., N. W., Washington, D. C. 20036.

Tennis-Badminton Guide. DGWS-AAHPER, 1201 16th St., N. W., Washington, D. C. 20036.

World Badminton. International Badminton Federation. H.A.E. Scheele, ed. 4 Madeira Avenue, Bromley, Kent, England.

Films

Assorted Badminton Films. R. Stanton Hales, 1143 Yale Ave., Claremont, Calif. 91711.

Audio-Visual Film Loops, Lifetime Sports Badminton. AAHPER Publications, 1201 16th St., N. W., Washington, D. C. 20036.

Badminton Loops (16mm). Educational Productions, Inc., 915 Howard St., San Francisco, Calif. 94103.

Badminton Sports Techniques. Jim Poole and Margaret Varner Bloss. Athletic Institute, 805 Merchandise Mart, Chicago, Ill. 60654.

1967 All England Championships. Hashman-Takagi Match, J. Frank Devlin, Dolfield Road, Owings Mills, Md. 21117.

1969 U.S. Nationals Matches. Dr. Charles Thomas, Northwestern State College of Louisiana, Natchitoches, La. 71457.

1971 Canadian Open Finals (16mm).

1970 Canada vs. Denmark Match (16mm). (Separate Audio Tape). Canadian Badminton Association, 333 River Road, Ottawa, Ontario, Canada.

Selected Highlights—1973 U.S. Open Badminton Championships. (Video Tapes) The Travelers Insurance Companies, One Tower Square, Hartford, Conn. 06115.

Appendix:
Questions and answers

TRUE OR FALSE

t F   1. The thumb is placed on the back bevel of the handle for the forehand grip. (p. 6)

t F   2. The racket is held firmly in the palm of the hand. (p. 6)

t F   3. Backpedaling is the skill of moving backwards, peculiar to the game of badminton. (p. 9)

T f   4. A legal serve includes both the contact point and racket head being below the wrist. (p. 11)

T f   5. The serve is considered a defensive stroke because it is played underhand and must therefore be hit upwards. (p. 14)

t F   6. The overhead and forehand strokes originate high above the head with the wrist cocked. (p. 15)

T f   7. The trajectory of the attacking clear is lower than the defensive clear. (p. 17)

T f   8. The dropshot must be deceptive since its flight is slow. (p. 18)

T f   9. A smash played from the backcourt will have less downward angle than one played nearer the net. (p. 20)

t F 10. With proper timing it is not necessary to use shoulder and arm strength to obtain power. (p. 22)

T f 11. A drive may be played deep and fast or slower to midcourt, as well as crosscourt and down-the-line. (p. 23)

t F 12. The backhand clear is one of the easiest strokes to play and perfect. (p. 28)

t F 13. The half-smash has little value since it has less speed than a full smash. (p. 30)

T f 14. The round-the-head shot is a forehand shot played above the left shoulder. (p. 30)

t F 15. The driven serve is designed to push the receiver to the backcourt. (p. 32)

t F 16. Net shots are played with the same wrist and shoulder action as other shots for proper deception. (p. 33)

t F 17. Underhand shots are considered offensive shots because if deceptive they can keep the opponent from guessing their direction. (p. 35)

t F 18. "Holding the shuttle" is a deceptive technique useful against a slow-moving player. (p. 36)

t F 19. Repeated practice of each stroke separately tends to make a player lose the sense of game play. (p. 38)

T f   20. Practicing or playing with a player of like ability produces maximum benefits. (p. 38)

T f   21. Defensive play can be changed to offensive play depending on how well a stroke is executed and selected for use at the time. (p. 45)

t F   22. Angle of return in badminton is relatively unimportant since the court is only twenty feet wide. (p. 45)

t F   23. Crosscourt shots are best used when your opponent has not been drawn from the center position. (p. 47)

t F   24. Receiving serve in a diagonal (forward and back) stance allows the receiver to best cover the area to either side of him. (p. 47)

t F   25. In singles, the object is to move your opponent forward and back, using low serves, drives and dropshots. (p. 48)

T f   26. The half-smash and dropshot are often used to change defense into attack. (p. 30)

T f   27. A short clear should be returned with a smash or dropshot. (p. 34)

T f   28. In singles, the forehand side of the court may be vulnerable due to extra effort made compensating for weakness on the backhand. (p. 48)

t F   29. In doubles, teams should decide to play side-by-side or up-and-back without changing this formation during a point. (p. 51)

T f   30. Offense and defense are determined by the angle of the flight of the shuttle. (p. 45)

t F   31. The side-by-side formation lends itself best to attack. (p. 51)

T f   32. The up-and-back formation is best attacked with halfcourt shots. (p. 52)

t F   33. A high deep clear allows a team to assume the up-and-back positions. (p. 52)

T f   34. A well played halfcourt shot should lead both opponents to believe it is his shot to return. (p. 53)

T f   35. In mixed doubles, the woman should seldom make an attempt to return smashes and fast drives. (p. 54)

T f   36. Except when there is a set-up, the net player in doubles uses many halfcourt and net shots. (p. 57)

T f   37. There is a special formation to use in mixed doubles when the opposing man plays an overhead smash. (p. 57)

t F   38. The woman in mixed doubles should play the shuttle deep to the corners. (p. 54)

t F   39. In mixed doubles, the man should attempt to play most of the shots and direct them to the opposing woman. (p. 55)

t F   40. A balk is a deceptive and delaying movement used as a means of gaining a point. (p. 59)

t F   41. A carry is legal provided the flight of the shuttle is not drastically altered. (p. 59)

t F   42. A flick shot refers to shots played with an overhead stroke to surprise an opponent. (p. 60)

t F   43. A shuttle is "in play" when the serve crosses the net. (p. 61)

t F   44. The serving side wins the point when a let is called. (p. 61)

t F   45. The term "second service" means the team which did not serve first. (p. 62)

T f   46. When setting, the player reaching the tied score first has the option of setting. (p. 62)

T f   47. A shot played off the wood of the racket is legal. (p. 63)

T f   48. The heavier the shuttle, the faster it flies. (p. 64)

t F   49. A player losing the toss has no choices. (p. 65)

T f   50. In a three-game doubles match, players change ends when one team scores eight points. (p. 66)

t F   51. A doubles team may not change its order of service during the match. (p. 66)

T f   52. It is considered poor sportsmanship to change the speed of the shuttle by bending the feathers. (p. 76)

t F   53. A shuttlecock will have a slower flight at a high altitude and with low humidity. (p. 65)

t   F   54. Tournaments are played both indoors and outdoors at a sectional and
national level.   (p. 78)

COMPLETION

55. Identify the names of the following lines and areas of a badminton court.
    1. Right Service Court
    2. Side Boundary Line (doubles)
    3. Left Service Court
    4. Side Boundary Line (singles)
    5. Alley
    6. Long Service Line for Doubles
    7. Net
    8. Center Line
    9. Short Service Line
    10. Back Boundary Line and Long Service Line for Singles   (p. 2)

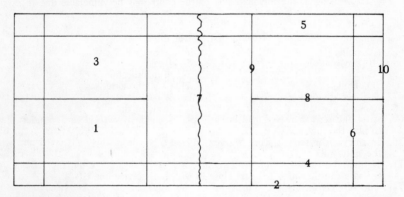

Complete the blanks:

56. Net heights	(5′ center), (5′ 1″ posts)	(p. 2)
57. Shuttle weights	(73-85 grains)	(p. 2)
58. Minimum ceiling height	(25′ above center of net)	(p. 2)

Give the required number of points for:

59. Ladies singles	(11 points)	(p. 3)
60. Mens singles	(15 points)	(p. 3)
61. Doubles	(15 points)	(p. 3)
62. Score set at 9 all	(3 points)	(p. 3)
63. Score set at 10 all	(2 points)	(p. 3)
64. Score set at 13 all	(5 points)	(p. 3)
65. Score set at 14 all	(3 points)	(p. 3)

66. On the court below draw and number the flight patterns for the following
strokes:
    1. Defensive Clear
    2. Attacking Clear
    3. Overhead Dropshot
    4. Smash
    5. High Singles Serve
    6. Low Doubles Serve
    7. High Doubles Serve
    8. Drive
    9. Hairpin Net Shot
    10. Underhand Clear

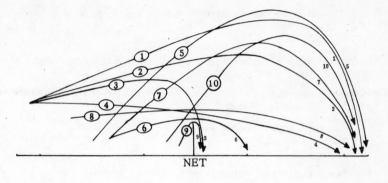

(p. 10)

Select one of the following letters to best answer the question.

A. point
B. service over
C. let
D. fault

E. second service
F. legal
G. disqualification
H. poor etiquette

67. A player attempting a serve, misses the shuttle completely. (C)   (p. 67)
68. A smash played by the server hits the very outside of the line. (A)   (p. 67)
69. After the serve a player inadvertently places one foot outside the boundary lines to play the shuttle. (F)   (p. 67)
70. In singles, the server's score is seven and he serves from the right court and wins the rally. (B)   (p. 67)
71. Neither the linesman nor the umpire can make a decision when the serving side served a shuttle which fell very close to the short service line. (C)   (p. 67)
72. The server contacts the shuttle below the waist and the racket head below the hand. (F)   (p. 67)
73. The server in singles takes a step before the shuttle is contacted. (B or D) (p. 68)
74. The receiver unsuccessfully returns a serve he claims was served before he was ready. (A)   (p. 68)
75. In doubles, the receiver receives serve in the wrong court and wins the rally. (C)   (p. 69)
76. In doubles, a player receives serve twice in succession and the serving side wins both rallies. (A)   (p. 69)
77. The receiver's partner is able to return a serve his partner cannot reach and scores a winner. (A or D)   (p. 69)
78. The shuttle passes between the net and net post and falls into the proper court. (D)   (p. 69)
79. A player contacts the shuttle on his side but the racket head carries over the net. (F)   (p. 69)
80. A player touches the net on the follow through of a smash after the shuttle hit the floor. (F)   (p. 69)
81. The server hits an opponent with a shuttle which is going out. (A)   (p. 70)
82. The net player is able to return a smash by ducking below the net and putting his racket up to intercept the shuttle. (D)   (p. 70)
83. In mixed doubles, the server places himself behind his partner in order to hide the shuttle from the receiver. (D)   (p. 70)
84. A player consults his coach between games. (G)   (p. 70)
85. A player calls no shot or fault whenever it occurs during play. (H)   (p. 73)
86. In doubles, with the score 8-7, the first server serves and the serve hits the top of the net and goes into the correct court. (F)   (p. 67)

Index